USINE:
SAINT·DENIS (SEINE)

Mich

L'AUTOMOBILE
MAJOLA
FRANCHIT SANS BRONCHER TOUS LES OBSTACLES

MOTORING
THE GOLDEN YEARS

A PICTORIAL ANTHOLOGY

COMPILED BY

RUPERT PRIOR

WITH A FOREWORD BY

CYRIL POSTHUMUS

WITH ILLUSTRATIONS FROM

THE KHACHADOURIAN GALLERY

BLOSSOM

H.C. BLOSSOM LTD.

FOR R.O. DIXON, AS PROMISED.

First published in Great Britain 1991
By H.C. Blossom Ltd.
6/7 Warren Mews,
London W1P 5DJ.

ISBN 1 872532 14 4

This book was conceived, edited, designed and produced by
Morgan Samuel Editions,
11 Uxbridge Street, London W8 7TQ.

Typesetting by Sprint Reproductions Ltd, London
Film separations by Toppan Printing Co. (HK) Ltd., Hong Kong
Printed and bound in Hong Kong

CONTENTS

FOREWORD

By Cyril Posthumus

One might liken an anthology to a series of windows in time, through which the reader peeps to see what goes on inside. The windows may vary in size and clarity, some affording a mere glimpse within, while others offer a broad, clear view. Those windows constitute history, and whatever Henry Ford said about it being "bunk", history remains the record of man's endeavour. Rupert Prior's anthology, MOTORING: THE GOLDEN YEARS, extracts gold from the absorbing history of the motor car, and from the early races that have helped it to develop muscles and reliability. While some critics have viewed racing as a trivial digression from the evolution of the car, others see it as it was, and still is – a vital, fascinating sport and an invaluable test-bed for car design.

When the first motor cars displaced the horse and sent man off on an enthralling new tack, it was inevitable that he would challenge other motoring adventurers, if only to "Show that blighter up at the manor what a decent motor can do", or to resolve the eternal question, "How fast will it go?". It was unfortunate that Britain's narrow-minded lawmakers of the late 19th century chose to impose a petty speed limit of 12mph upon early British motorists. Hamstrung as it was, Britain could thus contribute little to the early evolution of the car, whereas in Germany, France, Austria and Belgium, racing was an important developer of stronger, faster motor cars, beginning in short, sharp sprints on suitable stretches of road, and climaxing in full-blooded town-to-town road races.

Racing brought stress and strain to the car, testing its engine and other delicate parts. Rough, bumpy roads loosened nuts and bolts, broke frames, cracked radiators, fractured petrol, oil and water connections, broke wheels and steering links, punctured tyres, and wrought other damage. Experience, however, taught motorists many effective repairs, while manufacturers successful in racing gained orders for new cars from discerning enthusiasts. Stress also visited the drivers. At high speed through dust, mud or rain, intrepid "speedmen" had to learn how to read the roads, sense the well-being of their engines, and nurse vehicles over hundreds of miles. Luxuries such as oil-pressure and water-temperature gauges were initially unknown; electricity was fickle and batteries fragile, while tyres were a constant worry on the loose, stony roads of the time.

Yet those early races helped evolve the conventional road car, and by around 1905 production car design had settled to a pattern that included front-mounted four-cylinder engine with automatically operated inlet valves, a three-speed separate gearbox, and chain final drive. A few years more and road racing had developed higher compression engines with side-by-side valves, shaft final drive, better brakes, and other refinements, most of which were passed on to improve road cars. Meanwhile the long French Grand Prix series of races began in 1906, and cars grew larger engines, many with pushrod overhead valves; others still further advanced with single overhead camshafts, while four-speed gearboxes became the rule rather than the exception.

In those memorable French contests, first France (Renault), then Italy (Fiat), Germany (Mercedes), then France again (Peugeot) emerged triumphant, whereas England's showing was modest. In 1907, however, a wealthy architect named Locke King laid down a new and sensational banked race track at Brooklands, in Surrey, where cars and drivers could disport themselves on the concrete, developing high-speed stamina for man and machine. From there, British makes moved on to tackle Continental events and it was in 1912 that the British-built Sunbeams scored a magnificent 1-2-3 victory in the up-to-3

litres Voiturette class of the French GP at Dieppe, using four-cylinder side-valve production-based engines.

Some special note should be made of that other great man-made circuit, Indianapolis, the famous brick-paved 2½-mile oblong speedway with its four-banked corners, built in 1909. America's most spectacular motor race, the Indianapolis 500 Miles, inaugurated in 1911, was resumed in 1919 after a two-year break, and subtitled "The Victory Stakes". American "Howdy" Wilcox (Peugeot) was the first home in this classic event.

Four years later, two Sunbeams carried off the first two places in the 1923 French GP itself, the winning car being driven by Henry Segrave, who rated as one of Britain's star drivers of the 1920s. Other masters in the fascinating international battleground of Grand Prix racing included the Italian Nazarro (Fiat), the German Lautenschlager (Mercedes), and the Frenchman Boillot (Peugeot), all of whom twice won the Grand Prix. Other top-liners included Szisz (Renault), Goux (Ballot and Bugatti), Irish-American Murphy (Duesenberg), Campari and Ascari (Alfa Romeo), Bordino and Wagner (Fiats), Benoist (Delage) and others, all contributing to the grand scenario of motor racing.

The quest for success in the later '20s became so keen that manufacturers overspent, and racing went through a bleak period which coincided with the Wall Street crash of 1929 and subsequent world slump. Some race organisers chose to promote less expensive sports car events instead of Grands Prix, examples including the Ulster TT, Irish GP and the Belgian 24 Hours. Competing sports cars such as Bentley, Alvis, Mercedes-Benz, Riley and Lea-Francis scored significant successes. The name "Bentley", for instance, became synonymous with Le Mans, France's great 24-hour Endurance GP, by

winning it five times; in the late 1920s, the race was much enlivened by the entry of American cars. In the 750cc class of racing in Britain, tiny Austin Sevens and MG Midgets won frequently.

The liquidation in 1931 of the Bentley concern was to raise the question: "Was racing too expensive?". However, a lifting of the economic gloom brought fresh contenders such as Bugatti, Alfa Romeo and Maserati, while in 1934 Britain's new 1½-litre ERAs blossomed forth in the international 1½-litre Voiturette class, scoring many first class races at home and away, and providing a new training ground for young British drivers. That same 1934 brought significant changes in the Grand Prix world. Dictator Mussolini had shown Italy a way to enhance national prestige by encouraging Alfa Romeo and Maserati to win races; indeed, by ordering them to do so with his celebrated telegrams! His example was taken up by Hitler of Germany, who foresaw the benefits in national prestige to be gained by winning major races, and encouraged the German manufacturers Mercedes-Benz and Auto-Union to build new racing machines to represent the Reich, by the subtle offer of subsidies and bonuses.

First appearing in May, 1934, the new German cars, proved sensational in design and effect, and were virtually unassailable for the next six years. In events held all over Europe, and further afield, Germany's raucous "Silver Arrows" totally dominated Grand Prix racing, the two marques jointly scoring 52 major victories. Ironically, their victory march was broken only by Hitler himself when hostilities began in September 1939, and motor racing ceased.

Cyril Posthumus
January 1991
Surrey, England.

In the early
Edwardian age there
was perhaps no make
of motor car more
generally favoured by
aristocracy and the
public alike than
those produced by
Comte (later Marquis)
de Dion and M.
Bouton.

FIRST STEPS

How it all began:

the birth of a new era of speed

A F.I.A.T. poster of 1927 by Giuseppe Romano, born in Sicily in 1905 and architect of the Fiat corporate image for decades.

WEDDING
1898

Last week a marriage was celebrated between the Hon. Eleanor Rolls and the son of Lady Margaret Shelly, at Ennismore Gardens Church.

We need hardly say that the bride is the sister of the Hon. C. S. Rolls, who is well known throughout the autocar world as an enthusiastic follower of the latest form of recreative locomotion. Therefore, it is not surprising to hear that Mr Rolls drove friends to the church in an elegant motor victoria, and also in the procession afterwards back to the residence of his family at Rutland Gate, where a reception attended by some four or five hundred guests was held.

So far as we know, this is the first time (though it certainly will not be the last) in which an autocar has been used by people of independent position in connection with a wedding of any note.

CURIOSITIES OF RECORD BREAKING
By R. King-Farlow

Motor speed records owe their inception to the French journal, La France Automobile, which, on December 18th, 1898, organised the first timed kilometre trials, at Achères. The course was over two kilometres, cars being timed over the distance from both standing and flying starts. The meeting, which was greatly marred by rain, attracted four competitors, a 40-h.p. 1,450-kilogram Jeanteaud electric machine, two 9-h.p. Bollées and a little 1¾-h.p. 95 kilo De Dion tricycle. The big electric car, driven by the Count de Chasseloup-Laubat, carried off the honours with averages of 30.7 and 39.3 m.p.h. over the standing and flying kilometre respectively.

Immediately after the first meeting, Cammile Jenatzy issued a challenge to the Count to a match between their electric cars to be held on the Achères course within a month. The challenge was accepted and took place on January 17th, 1899. On his first run over the flying kilometre, Jenatzy recorded 41.4 m.p.h., thus taking the record, but Chasseloup-Laubat quickly regained his crown with a speed of 43.7 m.p.h. Ten days later Jenatzy, not content, made a solo run and clocked 49.93 m.p.h., to which Chasseloup-Laubat replied with 58.25 m.p.h., a few weeks after. Jenatzy then got down to the matter in real earnest, and built the first specially designed record-breaker, the direct ancestor of all Bluebirds. This was the famous "Jamais Contente", a freak electrical machine with a cigar-shaped body to lessen wind resistance, and almost microscopic wheels. As the bulk of the machinery was carried exposed below the chassis, and as most of the driver's body protruded into the air, the elaborate attempt at streamline lost much of its force, but, nevertheless, the "bolide" achieved its object, and, by recording 34 seconds dead over the kilometre, gave to its designer and driver the honour of being the first man to record a speed of a mile-a-minute and 100 k.p.h., the exact figures being

Fiat Mod.520 1927 by J.Le Breton. Soon after its founding in 1899, Fabbrica Italiana di Automobili Torino was present on land, sea and air. This premier Italian firm has been known as Fiat since 1906.

65.79 m.p.h. (105.88 k.p.h.). The "Jamais Contente" is still preserved in the Musée des Voitures at Compiegne.

The first official holder of the World's Mile record, as recognised by the A.I.A.C.R., was Henri Fournier, who clocked 75.95 m.p.h. over the distance with an 80-h.p. Mors at Dourdan in November, 1902. Fournier's record stood till January, 1904 when the great Henry Ford himself, driving a 70-h.p. Ford,

11

Walter Thor, a member of the Salon des Artistes Francais is best known for his humourous automobile posters of the early years of the century.

The Queen Mother, then the Duchess of York, talking to Elsie Wisdom at Brooklands Motor Course in 1932. The Duke, later King George VI, is to the right.

recorded (much to his amazement, the story goes) a speed of 91.37 m.p.h. on the frozen Lake St. Clare, Michigan. Ford's car "No. 999", was a four-cylinder monstrosity of nearly 18-litres, with no gears, no body whatsoever, and incredibly frail-looking wire wheels. Brakes were apparently non-existent to judge from the photographs, but as Henry survived his ordeal there must have been some way of reducing speed. Perhaps he threw out an anchor. Ford's record was very short-lived, for only a week or two later came the second Daytona Beach Record Meeting at which W. K. Vanderbilt, donor of the Vanderbilt Cup, clocked 39 seconds over the mile, equivalent to 92.30 m.p.h.

Since 1904 Daytona, or Ormonde-Daytona to give it its earlier title, has been the centre of land speed record work. Only last season, after 32 years, has its supremacy been challenged by the Utah Salt Beds. The record has been broken there no less than sixteen times. No other spot can claim anything like such popularity. The park at Achères has six records to its credit, Pendine Sands and the Nieuport – Ostend road following with five each, and Dourdan three. Incidentally, the true history of the Land Speed Record is extremely difficult to trace, and indeed has never, I believe, been officially registered. Details regarding the timing of the earlier attempts are hard to come by, particularly those held at the Daytona Meetings.

The first car to record a speed of 100 m.p .h. was a 100-h.p. Gobron-Brillié, running on alcohol fuel and driven by Rigolly. On July 27th, 1904, Rigolly covered a kilometre on the Nieuport – Ostend road in 21.6 seconds, equalling 103.56 m.p.h. This car was a remarkable vehicle, built on the usual Gobron principle with two horizontally opposed pistons to each cylinder. Its chief claim to fame, apart from its record, was its extraordinarily long life, in an age when the racing car of one season was almost invariably obsolete by the next. The old Gobron, however, was still running, and running well, up to 1907, when Rigolly drove in the second Grand Prix de l'A.C.F.

MORE CURIOSITIES OF EARLY RACING
By R. King-Farlow

The Circuit du Sud Ouest of 1900 was won by the Chevalier Réné De Knyff, who brought his Panhard to the finishing line 47 minutes in advance of his nearest rival, apparently an exceptionally easy win. In actual fact, it was not so easy, for the words "brought his car to the finishing line" must be taken absolutely literally. Shortly before the end of the course, De Knyff's water pump broke. He managed to struggle on with the car boiling furiously and enveloped in steam and fumes, but broke down on the line itself, being utterly unable to move another inch.

Nowadays, whenever the regulations of a race allow lady drivers to compete, the lay press informs us that for the first time in history women are "challenging" men in an international event, or that Brooklands is staging a novelty in the shape of a race specially for women drivers. In actual fact the first appearance of a women driver in a really big event was as far back as 1901, when Madame Du Gast piloted her 20-h.p. Panhard over the 687 miles from Paris to Berlin at an average speed of 26.9 m.p.h., arriving 33rd out of the 120 starters. Madame Du Gast also drove successfully through the famous Paris-Madrid race of 1903, arriving at Bordeaux, where the race was stopped, 77th of the 175 cars that started. On this occasion she drove a 30-h.p. De Dietrich. So far as Brooklands events are concerned, the first ladies' race held there was at the Midsummer Meeting of 1908 when Miss M. Thompson, driving Mr. O. S. Thompson's Austin "Pobble", won a three-lap handicap at 71 m.p.h., Mrs. Locke King being a very close second in her Itala.

No survey of old-time racing would be complete without some mention of Gabriel's wonderful run in the ill-fated Paris-Madrid race of 1903. Driving a 70-h.p. Mors Gabriel, starting 82nd among a field of 227 cars and motor-cycles, arrived at Bordeaux third, having passed 79 other cars on the way. His average speed for the 342 miles, excluding controls, was 65.3 m.p.h.

Yet More Curiosities Of Early Racing
By R. King-Farlow

In 1903 America made its first bid for international motor racing honours, by entering for the Gordon-Bennett Cup. The Automobile Club of America issued an appeal for entries to make up the trio permitted to compete; rather to their surprise, five names were sent in. Of these, one, Winton, claimed precedence, having sent in his challenge to the Cup Committee before the A.C.A. themselves challenged. This claim was allowed, but a special series of speed trials was announced to decide which of the other four entrants should have the two remaining places in the team.

Little was known of the cars entered, save that each was rumoured to be more powerful, more speedy and more mysterious than the others. Unhappily the trials themselves proved an almost complete fiasco. The course was a six-mile stretch of macadam on Long Island, close to the circuit where the Vanderbilt Cup was later held for several years. Only two racers turned up on the day fixed, and, after a few very unsatisfactory runs by these, the trials were postponed for a week. The second meeting, however, again saw but the same pair, who were accordingly awarded places in the Cup team. The nicest part of the whole business, however, was the fact that the timekeeping arrangements necessitated the official timekeeper travelling on the car itself, watch in hand. A delicious picture is conjured up of a present-day timekeeper crouching in terror in the spare seat of, say, the big Delage, or, as an alternative, perhaps, being towed behind in a specially constructed trailer. A beautiful thought, but perhaps a little arcadian.

* * *

The course for the 1903 Gordon-Bennett Cup, run in Ireland, was in the shape of a figure-of-eight, or rather of two rough circles, having one common side. History does not relate what steps were taken to prevent the simultaneous arrival from different directions on to the centre road of two ten-litre mon-

sters, neither blessed with more than a suspicion of brakes. Fortunately the situation did not arise, but there are undeniable possibilities about a course of this shape.

The timekeeping system employed in this event must have been about the most complicated ever attempted. Timekeepers swarmed at the start, at the entrance of each of the two "circles", and at each of the many controls. In all, no less than eighty-four chronographs were employed in the timing! Part of the system entailed a watch, which had been started when a competitor arrived at a control, being locked in a box and carried by a cyclist preceding the car to the end of the control, where it was stopped when the competitor was sent off again. I wonder how many of to-day's split-second experts would like to entrust their beloved Stauffers to a casual marshal on a push-bike!

Centre. Garretto depicts the pretty little French Amilcar, most popular with beret hatted sportsman.

14

An Emile Cardinaux poster of 1916, a successful year for the Swiss armaments and car manufacturer. They ceased automobile production in 1934.

F. Lutinger's "De Dietrich". France.c.1908.

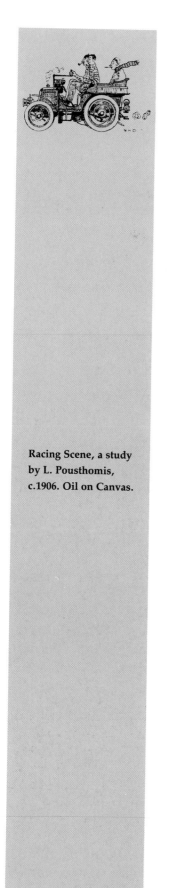

Racing Scene, a study by L. Pousthomis, c.1906. Oil on Canvas.

THE ST PETERSBURG – MOSCOW RACE OF 1908
By Arthur Bray

DUST! Dust in your eyes, your nose, your hair. Blinding dust mixed with the stones thrown up by the cars ahead; the stench of hot oil and the smoke belching from their exhausts and the whine of the driving chains in your ears. A straight road from St. Peters-burg to Moscow is 450 miles, never ending, with the hot morning sun in June glaring down on the dust alone, and the desolation of that long Russian highway. No side paths, a few trees clustered in places, and for miles on either side some sort of stubble fields on which those trailing dust clouds finally settled. An occasional village with quaint wooden shacks, peculiar-looking people with still more peculiar head gear and long boots

16

LPOUSTHOMIS

honour. Not much comfort, either; springs were hard, but we had spring dampers, in the form of rubber blocks under the spring clips which smote the frame with vigour when an extra deep pot-hole came along-but the suffering on a long journey, at speed!

A four-cylinder Bosch H.T. magneto sitting on the shelf in one of Charles Jarrott's store cupboards started my racing career! A magnificent 120 h.p. De Dietrich racer had been sent over in 1907 for him to attack the 50 and 100 miles world's records at Brooklands.

Hanging On! I say racer! The driver's seat was rather of the pedestal type whereby the grip of the hefty steering wheel set on a massive column gave one a certain confidence when proceeding over "broken" country, and thus enabled one to hold on or wedge one's self in the bucket seat which had a back (sic) support. The mechanic's seat, however, did not possess such "comforts" – merely a metal handle on the alleged dash and a sloping heel board, which also acted as a bracing piece to wedge one in, or assist in doing so, when momentarily leaving the ground, which frequently occurred on Brooklands and in Russia!

Let it not be thought that a mechanic's job in those days consisted of having a ride until "something happened". I would here and now disillusion readers on this point. Such luxuries as forced lubrication, oil cooling, mechanical petrol feeds, detachable wheels, and so forth, were quite unknown. There were always "odd jobs" to be done en route, such as pumping up the petrol with the long hand pump on the side, regulating the impossible array of drip-feed lubricators on the dash, since certain of them had to "stream" for the fast open road stuff, but be restricted to save oiling up the plugs when easing down to pass another competitor or entering controls. Then, of course, the driving chains had to have their spot of oil now and then from the oilcans, always kept handy at one's feet.

But back to the magneto! This certain De Dietrich was magnificent on the highways of France for road racing with occasional "easys", but when it was taken to the cement

seemingly much the worse for wear. No tar in those days, twenty-five years ago, to make the going easier.

It was just a race from one place to another, and you took everything as you found it. Yes, a mechanic's job was not always an enviable one, but much sought after. Racing cars were few and far between, and to sit in those funny little upright bucket seats with loose upholstery was, I suppose, considered an

17

A factory publicity photograph of the Mercedes victory in the 1938 Coppa Acerbo. In the terrific heat at Pescara the legendary Rudolf Caracciola was first home at 83.69 mph.

down Weybridge way, it definitely refused to function at speed after about four laps. Peculiar tappings in the engine caused the wiseacres many thoughtful moments, but I had ideas! This warrior was fitted with low-tension ignition which was then the standard for cars of this make – perfectly good for touring, thought I, but hardly for "period" racing round Brooklands.

The youthful enthusiasm of twenty years took me up to the sanctum of the great Charles with the request that for a maximum expenditure of £5 I might be allowed to increase the speed and endurance of the old "120" for twenty laps if necessary! His look might have frozen many an aspirant for that mechanic's seat, but, finally, a smile, probably at my cheek, and permission to try.

Success!! Forty-eight hours later, with four blanking plates over the old igniter holes and four new Bosch plugs and the magneto, I was driving the old warrior good and hearty round and round Brooklands, round and round again, and not a sign of pre-ignition. A little setting up on the magtiming, and then fifteen laps right off. I had driven a racing car at 92 m.p.h., faster than I had ever travelled before alone! Congratulations from Charles, and on the following days his personal tests to

confirm my report. "Yes, Bray, you were right."

But our troubles were not yet over, as tyres were far from perfect for those then "terrific" speeds. I think three different makes were tried before the final selection of Continent-

An original poster by Malzac from 1904. No other generation had been able to speed into the sunset with such easy hearts and minds as the early automobilists.

als, which enabled us, on the wintry day of February 5th, 1908, to lower the 50 miles world's record by nearly two minutes, thus beating H.C. Tryon's record with the 60 h.p. Napier which he had established on the previous January 2nd, nearly losing his life so doing when his car jumped over the embankment after the members' bridge.

The run was fairly uneventful, apart from the cold although, in spite of the weight of that old car, Brooklands was even in those days bumpy in places, and likewise the ride. One rather distinct memory remains of a torn glove and knuckles on my left hand when, in acknowledging the cheers of the small group of enthusiasts at the fork on passing the "50," my raised arm was swung over with the wind, and my hand made contact with the nearside driving chain, which was in rather close proximity.

A burst tyre on our off-side rear wheel at 721 miles put paid to our attempt on the "100" record, when we had several minutes in hand. Jarrott's excellent judgment here probably saved us from disaster-through a melange of driving chain and tyre-when he declutched and actually coasted from the fork to half way down the straight. Just the luck of the game, but 84 m.p.h. seemed fast then, sitting well up in the wind with no cowl or wind deflectors.

Russia – what visions this conjured up. In 1906 I had driven a car through to Paris, and had obtained my French driving licence. But Russia! And a road race for 450 miles. Surely this car, which had stood up well to the racketing of 72 miles around Brooklands flat out was equal to any roads in the world. Little we knew! Of course, bad roads were rumoured, so perhaps we should be prepared. Some gentleman was sure that, with gadgets known as lever spring suspension fitted to the shackles, we could withstand any bumps; other recommended friction shock-absorbers, rubber springs pads, two extra spring leavers. Yes, we would be prepared; we fitted the lot!

Just two and a half months after the record attempt I left by the sea with the car from Hull

and four days later the gold dome of the Cathedral of St. Isaac loomed out of the morning mist, and we were in St. Petersburg. A few days after Jarrott arrived, and again impressed on me that the roads were bad. Those spring clip nuts, shackle bolt nuts! Every nut and washer on that car was gone over with much sweating a dozen times; they were all tight!. Pope (Itala) came round to the garage one day and said that the only springs to stand those roads were made by Russian blacksmiths; his had all been changed. I showed him our array of precautions; he laughed, cynically I thought.

Can you imagine a race starting at 1.30 a.m.? To save the heat of the day, it may be an excellent time, but for obtaining well-needed sleep before an important race it is a miserable failure. On the Sunday morning previous to the start on the Monday, all the cars had to be assembled in the Riding School for inspection. A pleasant occupation on any Sunday morning with the added excitement of twenty or more racing engines being started up when the inspection was over, all their owners

19

being anxious to get out at once through the door. The air became steadily thicker with various languages, smoke and fumes from the large organ-type exhaust pipes, and Jarrott left me to my fate. With a few remarks passing in various languages, I managed to extricate the precious car in one piece from the melee, but I shall always remember that riding school.

The procession of cars to the start with their various types of bodies added colour to that June daybreak, but an added difficulty to the task of a driver of a racing car with a high gear ratio. By 1 a.m. it was fully light again, and all the entrants were on the line. We mingled such with great men as the game-little Duray, the previous year's winner, hook-nosed Rougier, both driving De Dietrichs; Hémery, and Pope, immaculate and cool with his Itala and Russian springs.

At 1.50 a.m. we were sent off, two behind Pope and eleventh in the line. What had that long, straight trail of 450 miles in store for us? How little we knew! Jarrott piled on the speed. At the first control we were to learn we had done second fastest time. It certainly felt like it. The map said it was a road; a track would have been a better description. It consisted of miles of loose stones, boulders occasionally, and then those wonderful little steep bridges at intervals, which at any speed over 40 lifted you right off your seat and dropped you again in a different position. How any car could stand that buffeting is still a mystery to me.

Then things began to happen. First one

shock absorber went, then two, three, four; after that the famous lever springs, rubber buffers, worse and worse. Under the car, Jarrott one side, I the other, tightening up spring bolts. My spanner slipped, and finding refuge in Jarrott's mouth, caused me to learn quite a lot about my ancestors hitherto unknown to me, until he climbed from under the car, and, finding a lot of open-mouthed, queer, bearded people gathered around, blew off the rest of his address on them.

Still, we persevered, once narrowly missing some tree trunks which local opposition had placed across the road. Difficulties were experienced in passing other cars, the chief being the terrible dust which blacked out everything ahead or astern. Jarrott's solution was a five-note horn, which it was intended I should blow. "Something uncommon, Bray, which will attract their attention."

I would have defied anyone to have blown that horn at speed on those roads and retained his front teeth. However, my solution was marbles. Yes, two pocketfuls. The modus operandi was to chase your man until you were right on his tail when he slowed down for one of the bridges, then shy a handful at the mechanic or driver, according to your aim. It worked well until the ammunition ran out, but by then cars were passing us!

Breaking Up!

Only one puncture did we have. and then the new Dunlop rims soon enabled us to get on the trail again. But still those roads. Stop-

pages became more frequent and the bumping worse as gradually the old car came adrift. We now had only one road spring intact; miles astern the detachable upholstery had become permanently detached, likewise my air cushion, and now nothing was left but the metal back and the square metal edge of the seat tool box to sit on. The steering column was showing signs of coming loose. but we had come a long way for this race, and we kept on at 20 miles per hour! We were paying dearly for the first control burst. and we had no Russian springs. C.J. kept looking down, I think really to see if I was still there, and each time I was in a different position, trying to find one unbruised part of my anatomy.

At last the end, thank heavens, at Valdai, about half way to Moscow. Tired and torn, battered and bruised, covered in dusty, oily filth from the road and the exhausts, and from our many visitations to the underneath of the car. Bloody hands, eyes streaming and bloodshot; C.J.'s massive frame so tired, as mine had been for miles, that neither of us could pull over the engine on half compression. We had finished, our race was over.

It seemed as though we were in the middle of Asia, with those long miles of desolation behind us, just a memory of perseverance against odds. One could not help but admire the driver for his skill and determination, with added sympathy for this disappointment. Not a soul in the village spoke our language, French, or German, and we had to get the car back to St. Petersburg and our weary bodies to Moscow.

During the day there slowly trickled into that village other disappointed and broken drivers and mechanics, until, in the station bar on the lonely railway, there was formed the Automobile Club de Valdai, with Charles Jarrott as president! I wonder how many throughout the universe could now answer the roll-call of membership of that select club. Perhaps the last memory of that famous race in which only ten finished out of twenty-nine starters was the portly form of C. J. and myself, dressed in our filthy racing kit, sweaters and skull caps, getting into the slow night train to Moscow, to find that Hémery had won the race at the colossal speed of over 51 m.p.h.

Geo Ham (Georges Hamel) started creating art works in the 1920's and by 1928 was a regular contributor to *L'Illustration*.

CHRYSLER

CURIOSITIES OF MOTOR RACING
By R. King-Farlow

From 1914 to 1918 Europe was a trifle too preoccupied with other matters to pay much attention to motor racing. However, the sport continued to flourish in America, occasionally with startling results. For example, in a race at San Diego, California, in January, 1915, Huntley Gordon had three tyres burst simultaneously. The car turned round a record number of times, finishing in a ditch, but the driver was unhurt.

Then in June of the same year came a 500 miles event at Maywood Speedway, Chicago. The winner was Harry Grant, with a Sunbeam, covering the course without a single stop, a performance that was unequalled until Hindmarsh's run with a Talbot in the 1930 B.R.D.C. event. Grant, however, came perilously near to missing his win. Two hundred yards short of the finishing line his 35-gallon fuel tank ran bone dry. Fortunately, nobody was close on his tail, and he was able to coast across the line to victory. It is interesting to compare Marcel Lehoux's luck in the final of this year's Grand Prix du Comminges. His Maserati also ran out of fuel 200 yards from the finish, when lying second. But in this case the road ran uphill just before the pits, and poor Marcel was done completely.

A third American excitement came in the Fort Snelling race in September, 1915. After a terrific duel Earl Cooper and Gil Anderson, both on Stutz cars, appeared to cross the line absolutely simultaneously. Luckily electrical timing was used, which gave the verdict in favour of Cooper, with a margin of five one-hundredths of a second, the closest finish ever recorded.

The first important post-War event was the 1919 Targa Florio. This race was won in sensational fashion by the French ace, Andre Boillot, with a Peugeot. Boillot's car was greatly handicapped by its small size, but its driver more than made up for this by driving with an abandon that shot him clean off the road no less than six times. Each time the car was hastily rescued and set going again,

WHITNEY STRAIGHT

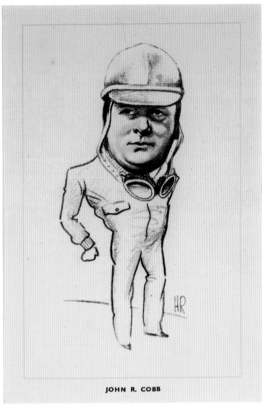

JOHN R. COBB

Whitney Straight, *left*, a wealthy American amateur who lent much colour to the racing scene and (*right*) an indelible hero, the imperturbable John Cobb.

undamaged. Finally, he arrived at the finish at top speed, to find the entire road blocked by spectators. Boillot braked madly, spun round three times, and shot into the grandstand, ten yards or so short of the line, the driver and mechanic being flung out. Willing assistants dragged the Peugeot back on to the road and thrust its dazed crew back into it, the car then crossing the line triumphantly in reverse. Loud cheers, and then panic ... would the car be disqualified for finishing backwards? Boillot and his mechanic, by now almost in a state of collapse, were again thrust back into the car, which then retired about twenty yards down the road, turned round and recrossed the finishing line in the orthodox manner. During the race Boillot carried out a distinctly novel refill. The car did not actually stop at its depot, but a can of fuel was thrown to the mechanic as he cruised by. The mechanic then waited till the car was descending a hill, opened the filler cap, poured in the contents of the can and had the pressure back to normal before the bottom of the hill was reached.

The year 1923 saw Brooklands stage its most original speed trial. The September Meeting was completely washed out by rain, making all racing impossible. However, to pass the time while waiting for it to clear, a bet was made between two members that it was possible to run up and down the Test Hill in a minute. "Alec", one of the Clubhouse waiters, a noted sprinter, was requisitioned, and accomplished the trip in 44 seconds, the applause being considerably louder than for any mere motor race. The only other Brooklands event that can compare with this novel hill climb was the golfing performance of John Cobb, who bet that he could drive a golf ball round the outer circuit in a certain number of strokes ... I forget the exact number. Before a large and notable gallery, Cobb accomplished his task, the incident laying further claim to history as being the only competition that has ever taken place at Brooklands on a Sunday. There is no record as to whether Cobb was fitted with an adequate silencer and fishtail to deal with language when balls darted into the sewage farm.

23

Centre. Josef Rudolf
Witzel was an
accomplished painter
and illustrator and a
regular contributor to
Jugend. This rare Audi
commission was
produced in 1912.

A Well-Known Woman Motorist Gives A Woman's View Of The 1934 Models

I think 1933 deserves a place in motor racing
history as the year when women were
allowed a fair share in a sport that previously
had almost entirely been a man's game. The
Brooklands experiment, by which women
drivers have been allowed to compete in the
ordinary handicap events at B.A.R.C. meetings, has proved a success, so I am told. At
the October meeting next week the first
mountain event for women is to be held.

Next year, so I hear, certain women drivers
will be allowed to participate in the 500 Miles
Race. So, with the exception of races organised by the R.A.C., the Isle of Man events,
and the "T.T.", women will be able to drive in
nearly every British event. That has been so,
of course, for some years on the Continent.

There has been considerable opposition,
but we have to thank the Clerk of the Course
at Brooklands, certain members of the committee of the B.R.D.C., and the racing committee of the B.A.R.C.

**What do women motorists think of the
1934 models?** Those I have seen and tried are
a definite advance on their prototypes. The
increase in price is more apparent than real; in
1934 you pay a little more and you get more
motor car. Body lines are more attractive, the
easy-change gear systems with which practically every car is fitted are an obvious selling
point. Springing, too, has received some
attention; two firms have models with
independent wheel suspension, Sunbeam
and Alvis, this year. Next year there will be
more.

I am sorry that there are so few firms that
standardise permanent jacks. I contend that
four wheel jacks are a necessity. Cars are
lower than ever, and with some of them it is a
physical impossibility to change a wheel
because there is no way of getting the jack
beneath the axle.

Manufacturers supply every car with a
starting handle, which is rarely used except
perhaps on sports models. Anyhow, in most
cases it is impossible to crank the engine; it is

easier to push the car. Yet the starting handle
is there in the tool box. I would rather have
four wheel jacks. Women drivers definitely
want them. In 1933 it should not be necessary
to grovel about on the road poking an
antiquated device beneath the axle.

Then there is the question of electrical
equipment. Believe it or not, but on a 1934
model not a month old one owner has had to
change the coil and six fuses. The car let him
down (it was a him this time) on the road at
night miles from anywhere twice. In less than
four weeks!

That shouldn't happen in 1933 and on 1934
models! Most motorists put reliability before
"improvements". The foregoing is all very
critical, I am afraid, but it represents what
women drivers are thinking and saying. The
cars are a definite advance, but to the woman
driver they do not represent anything like
finality.

Some day a motor manufacturer will let a woman driver, a comparative novice, try out his experimental models. And he will learn something of advantage.

I must confess to eavesdropping, but the conversation was so amazing as to warrant it. The customer in the next cubicle to mine at the hairdresser's had evidently some time before been telling the hairdressing assistant how she had complained to the garageman, where she parked her car each night, about the excessive amount of oil, in her opinion, which he had charged for and said that he had put in her car.

Having since moved to a house with its own garage, she had been very pleased to note the saving in money which had been spent on oil, until one day the poor ill-treated car had seized up solid for lack of lubricant. The owner evidently was amazed and indignant that the car had not just obligingly run out of oil, as it would of petrol; then she would have refilled it and all would have been well.

A very excellent feature of the Talbot range, which should appeal to women drivers, is that by pouring oil into the engine sump the entire lubrication, with the exception of the back axle, is attended to. There is no need to look at the gear box, spring shackles, universal joints, or the other usual points needing lubrication. They are all fed automatically from the engine. Such a saving in time and trouble!

A silver pewter (a.k.a. Zin in Germany) inkwell made by W.M.F. from 1910 to 1914.

25

Shell racing
achievements.

IT WAS A FAMOUS VICTORY!
Le Mans, 1935

Superlative drivers at the wheels of superlative cars are an asset, admittedly in a long-distance road race, but this year at Le Mans, our own drivers and cars were faced with foreign competition of almost equal calibre.

What, then, was the factor which led to Great Britain's sensationally sweeping victory – in fact, her complete annihilation of her rivals?

A slight superiority of driver perhaps; a definite superiority of cars and organisation certainly; but above all, in our opinion our national temperament.

Imagine setting forth on a 24 hours race, about seven hours of which must be completed in darkness, after the course has just been deluged by a torrential storm, with the almost certain expectancy of foul weather conditions throughout.

Surely no greater test of determination to triumph over discomfort and difficulty could be devised!

That the British contingent at Le Mans triumphed so completely in the face of such conditions, is no less tribute to the grit typical of the nation they represented, than it is to their own intrepidity and to the excellence of their cars.

Nevertheless, whilst justly congratulating our drivers and manufacturers on their success, let us not overlook the element of luck which (in fairness, one must admit) went far to make this success possible.

Our sincere sympathy goes out to Helde and Stoffel whose Alfa-Romeo would almost certainly have won, had it not been for an inexcusable error on the part of the timekeepers or announcer.

Towards the end of the race, the winning Lagonda was running at reduced speed and was passed by Helde, whom the Lagonda drivers had displaced from the lead between nine and ten o'clock in the morning.

The loud-speakers announced that Helde was now back in the lead and British hopes suffered a terrible set-back. Accordingly, Helde was signalled from his pit to slow down, which he did, and it was not until 11 minutes before the finish that the announcer casually corrected his previous statement, and pointed out that Helde actually was not in the lead at all, but lay one lap behind the British car.

By then, of course, all chance of Helde catching the Lagonda was dashed; whereas, had the previous wrong information not been broadcast, as a result of which his pit slowed him, the result might have been very different.

Undoubtedly, Helde deserves our sympathy and this we offer him sincerely, but with the one reservation, that his own pits timekeepers should have been sufficiently au fait with the position not to have been misled by the false announcement.

No fewer than fifty-eight cars were drawn up in echelon at the start at 4.0 p.m. on Saturday, June 15th, and so far down the road did the line of cars stretch, that three repeater flags had to be used to give the starting signal.

At the fall of the flag all got away, with the exception of two French cars which, however, were but momentarily delayed.

Hon. Brian Lewis, driving Earl Howe's 2.3 litre Alfa-Romeo led at the end of lap 1, closely followed by a pack of other competitors.

Later in the race (on its 29th lap, to be exact) this car put up the fastest lap of any car this year, at 86.75 m.p.h.

Not long after this start, however Sommer (Alfa-Romeo) took the lead, as Lewis was forced into the pits with distributor trouble.

From this moment until shortly after 11.0 p.m., Sommer held on to the lead, but the British cars were forcing too hot a pace for him, and as a result the Alfa blew up.

At this point the ultimate winner took the lead.

Arthur Fox's 4½-litre Lagonda which was being brilliantly driven by J. S. Hindmarsh, one of Great Britain's most experienced long-distance drivers and Luis Fontes, winner of the Jubilee Day International Trophy Race at Brooklands.

Lewis on the Alfa-Romeo now occupied

fifth place, and it was shortly before this time that T. S. Fotheringham, co-driver with C. Penn-Hughes, on one of the Aston-Martins, had a crash from which he was lucky to escape with his life – bruised and shaken as he was.

It appears that Fotheringham had taken White House bend a shade too fast, with the result that his car slid, out of control, to the bank which it mounted bouncing off across the road where it overturned on top of the driver who, however, was fortunate enough to escape with comparatively slight injuries.

At about the time Fotheringham was involved in these hair-raising convolutions, S. H. Newsome shot off the road at Arnage without personal injury, but necessitating the retirement of his Riley.

Two other misfortunes overtook Rileys during the race. One of these was when the car which Freddie Dixon and Cyril Paul were driving burst into flames at the pits and had to be withdrawn, and the other was shortly after 9 o'clock on Sunday morning, when the car which had been driven extremely fast throughout by Sebilleau and Delaroche, and had always been prominently placed, got into a broadside skid near Arnage and overturned – fortunately without injury to the driver.

The Lagonda was still leading at a few minutes before 2 a.m. on Sunday, when it developed trouble which forced it into the pits.

This stop cost Fox's car four places and the lead passed back to Earl Howe's Alfa-Romeo, followed in second place by the Veyron and Labric (Bugatti), with the Stoffel and Helde (Alfa-Romeo) third.

At dawn on Sunday, the weather showed signs of improving, but the road was still wet, and it was then that Elwes executed his tail-first slide after passing the Grand Stands, hitting the parapet and continuing broadside for a considerable distance.

Again the driver escaped unscathed, but the tail of his car was sadly crumpled, and had subsequently to be removed before the car could continue.

Earl Howe's Alfa-Romeo maintained the

lead until, at about 5.30 a.m., a broken piston put it out of the race.

This let Helde up into the lead, but by this time Hindmarsh, on the Lagonda, had worked his way back into second place, meanwhile, Dr. Benjafield's and Sir Ronald Gunter's Lagonda appeared in third place; but it did not occupy this position long as, between 6 a.m. and 7 a.m. it dropped back to fifth position.

At 8 a.m. Helde still led Hindmarsh by a fraction over two minutes, but now a new British challenge was becoming material, the Aston-Martin of C. E. C. Martin and Charles Brackenbury coming up into third position.

At a few minutes before 10 a.m. the Lagonda passed the Alfa-Romeo to go up into the lead, the plucky little Aston-Martin was still third and going great guns, this car by

28

Unrecorded artwork for Hotchkiss who, with the type A.R., produced the chassis of a vintage car at its superlative best.

now also having established a very considerable lead in the separate race, run simultaneously, for the Coupe Biennial.

As the results show, the order of the first three in the general classification at the end was the same as at 10 a.m., although right up to the last minute the ultimate issue was in doubt, as Fontes was making frequent pit-calls to report ever-dwindling oil-pressure, and each time he was told to proceed gingerly – a nerve-wracking experience at the end of a long-distance race, when the second car is right on one's tail.

Little mention has been made in the above notes of the progress of the Biennial Cup Race, as, really, after an excellent start by the Singers, which, however, was not maintained owing to starter trouble at the pits, the Aston-Martins dominated this race; but it must be

recorded that the Singer and Riley entries fought a pitched battle throughout for second place, the former ultimately beating their rivals to it by a figure of merit difference of only .02.

The French Grand Prix at Rheims 1938. Brauchitsch leads the way from Lang and Caracciola. Brauchitsch was the winner in a 1, 2, 3, victory for the Mercedes team.

29

V.M. Lorant heralds
the opening of the
Negresco. Society
lived well. The rich
drove Daimlers, Rolls-
Royces and the
Lanchester ("at 50
mph you can knit
comfortably").

J. Matiano's
"St. James's Levee". A
watercolour and
gouche illustration for
*Illustrated London
News*.

MASTER OF THE KING'S HORSE
1937

The King owns the finest fleet of private motor
cars in the world, and strangely enough the
official in supreme charge of them is the
Master of the Horse! The late King Edward VII
was the first British sovereign to own a motor
car, and it was he who decided that the new
type of vehicle was to come under the juris-
diction of the officer whose post for centuries
had been traditionally associated with the
royal horses and carriages.

The Marquis de Soveral, King Edward's
intimate friend, solemnly suggested that a
new official to be called Master of the Petrol
Horse should be appointed. King Edward VII
made his first trip in a motor car, a 12 h.p.
Daimler, in 1899, the driver being the late
Lord Montagu of Beaulieu.

The King enjoyed the experience so much

that he purchased a number of cars a few months after Queen Victoria's death, chiefly Daimler and Mercedes models. It was Edward VII who ordered the Royal Mews at Buckingham Palace to be altered to accommodate cars, a procedure which gravely upset the Victorian coachmen and stable lads.

Those who imagine that the suggestion that a Coronation motor coach should be used at the approaching ceremony in May is new or novel should be reminded that the idea was put before Edward VII 35 years ago! That tactful monarch made it known that he was quite willing to adopt the suggestion, provided that a car "without noticeable vibration, noise, smell or vapour" could be guaranteed! This was too much for the early motoring pioneers to promise!

Royal patronage

The motorist of to-day owes much to the four British sovereigns of this present century. Edward VII, by his patronage 35 years ago, did much to break down the general antagonism to the motor car. He agreed to become Patron of the Automobile Exhibition in the Crystal Palace in 1903 – the pioneer of the modern Motor Show – and conferred in 1907 the prefix "Royal" to the Automobile Club founded in 1897. The first British sovereign to motor took a great personal interest in the transformation of the Royal Mews at Buckingham Palace, Windsor Castle and Sandringham to house the new royal cars, and that they are to-day the most up-to-date garages in Europe is largely due to the modern outlook and foresight of the present King's grandfather and his Master of the Horse, the Duke of Portland.

M.O.H. – horse-lover

There is something ironic in the fact that the first M.O.H. to have a fleet of motor cars under his supervision should be that great lover of horses, still, at 80, happily with us. The Duke would probably be the first to admit that in those early days the real Master of the Horse, so far as actually looking after the cars was concerned, was Stamper, a motoring pioneer, who was given by King Edward VII the title of "Motor Mechanic" and put in working charge of all the royal cars.

The Earl of Granard, who succeeded the Duke of Portland as Master of the Horse, and continued with a brief break in that post until the death of King George V, witnessed the gradual evolution of the high-wheeled "smelly" cars to the magnificent modern luxury vehicles of to-day. In his official capacity he always kept the royal motor fleet up to date, and this tradition is being ably maintained by his successor, the 37 years' old Duke of Beaufort, who was appointed to the post last year.

Although a noted huntsman, the Duke is a keen motor car enthusiast and since his appointment he has made a thorough inspection of all the royal cars. It must be remembered that the King, in addition to providing cars for himself and his family, has to put a good number at the disposal of his personal suite and staff.

The Master of the Horse has three cars for

L'ÉLÉGANTE
MOTEURS DE DION
6·9·12 Chevaux
2,900 FCS
TÉLÉPHONE : 565·30
MÉTROPOLITAIN : Obligado.
J.B. MERCIER – 6. Rue St. Ferdinand

Motorists protected from the elements. Bonnets had to stay on in the wind, keep out the dust *and* look decorative!

31

"Vitesse" by Réné Lalique who established himself in Paris as a goldsmith and jeweller before specialising in glassware.

Tyre-shaped decanter with cork seal and lid manufactured in sterling silver. Matching ashtray. English and dated 1907.

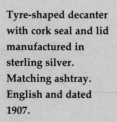

his own public and private use and the King's private secretary has at least two. Then there are equerries, high Household officials and servants, each of whom have their own special car in the Royal Mews. As can be imagined, the upkeep of the King's cars costs a considerable sum every year, and control of the money is entirely in the hands of the Master of the Horse, who is allowed a certain sum per annum out of the King's State allowance. No car can be bought, repaired or "scrapped" for the Royal Household without the authority of the M.O.H. or his acting deputy, the Superintendent of Royal Mews.

The departure and return of every car in the Mews is minutely recorded – "joy riding" by royal employees is absolutely impossible! Royal cars are purchased through dealers in the ordinary way and usual list prices are paid for them. Every day the office of the Master of the Horse is flooded with circulars from motor selling firms in Britain, the Continent, and the United States, but generally a select list of about half a dozen London car dealers fulfils all the requirements of the Master of the Horse.

Inspection

If the King or any member of the Royal family or Household wishes to examine a new model, the dealer selected is requested to send a car to the Mews for inspection or perhaps trial. On these occasions the M.O.H. is always present, and unless the sovereign intimates his desire to acquire a car on show, the "Master" can decline, if he so decides, to sanction any purchase. Apart from the King he is the sole arbiter in the matter.

The present M.O.H., the Duke of Beaufort, likes going personally to motor showrooms and this last few months he has been "spotted" during more than one of these expeditions! Not so long ago he and H.R.H. The Duke of Kent, President-in-Chief of the British Racing Drivers' Club, were seen gazing into a certain window of a Portland Place showroom! The Duke of Beaufort, of course, is a very intimate friend of the Royal Family and is married to Lady May Cambridge, niece

of Queen Mary and cousin of the King. He is a modern young man in every way and already he has introduced many reforms in the Royal Mews. The accommodation for cars has been extended, more petrol pumps have been installed, and some of the slipways have been levelled and improved. A number of car models never before seen in the Mews have been added by him to the "fleet" and they are not all fashionable ones either!

Every chauffeur's ambition

A number of elderly drivers have been pensioned off and young men put in their places. To secure a post in the Royal Service is the ambition of every private chauffeur in London, who is aware of the excellent working conditions in the Mews. Every morning scores of applications for jobs, even as car washers, reach the Master of the Horse. Tests for prospective royal drivers are very severe, which perhaps explains why so few, if any, accidents or mishaps ever happen to any of the King's cars. The post of the Master of the Horse is no sinecure for it carries a great responsibility. Yet there are very few motor car lovers who would not jump at it!

A Walter Thor poster, circa 1906.

Cottin-Desgouttes took part in the early Paris-Nice trials, made a fine 10½-litre Edwardian and finally ceased production in 1929.

33

"Experienced nannie wants situation, used to children and cars; quite willing to act as CHAUFFEUSE in her spare time." – Daily paper advertisement. A member of the Chauffeurs' Union says that "it is this sort of nannie which gets his goat".
1905

A Designer Who Drives
An Interview With Herr Uhlenhaut, Chief Technical Engineer of Mercedes Benz By Brian P. W. Twist 1938

It has been said that a thing is not worth doing unless it is done well, and this excellent maxim has been applied, with all the efforts of German thoroughness, to the racing activities of Mercedes-Benz, whose vast equipe, if all goes well, will be seen at Donington in to-day's Grand Prix.

Amateur motor racing is all very well in its way, and is great fun for the competitors. The great spectacle provided by formula Grand Prix racing cannot be achieved, however, without the most intense organisation and preparation, and by the expenditure of a tremendous amount of money. There is the same difference between a full Grand Prix and the type of race usually seen in this country as between the Cup Final and a Saturday afternoon club match.

Ramifications
Mercedes-Benz have been racing ever since the game started, and their equipe has been gradually built up to its present eminence. Besides their remarkable team of drivers, which includes, to everyone's pride, an Englishman, their experimental department is of enormous size, numbering several hundred men. Not all these are engaged on the racing side, but racing plays a very big part in the department's programme. O si sic alii!.

On the racing side, the chief of the experimental department is a young man, Uhlenhaut, and for the last few years he and other technical experts have accompanied the team to the races in various countries, in order that their theories should not be confined to the drawing-board, but that they should have actual practical experience of what happened to the cars that they had built.

Uhlenhaut supervises their building, and is responsible for any modifications that may become necessary, either in the test shop or on the actual scene of a race.

He is also one of the very few technical men in any country who is also a first-class racing driver. Often during practice for an event he will put in nearly as many laps as the actual members of the team testing out carburation, springing, steering, and the manifold other problems which arise in the preparation of the cars.

During the practice period for the German Grand Prix, Uhlenhaut put in a lap of the Nurburg Ring in 10 mins. 32.4 secs., at no less than 80.6m.p.h. This time was only two seconds longer than the best practice lap put in by the redoubtable Hans Stuck, and only 23 seconds longer than the best lap made during the race itself by Richard Seaman.

Thus, if a driver comes in with a criticism of some point in the handling of the cars, Uhlenhaut does not have to guess at the trouble, but off comes his coat, he dons a helmet and goggles, and he is away tearing round the circuit at a speed almost equal to that of the ace drivers themselves.

The late T. Murray Jamieson, designer of the overhead camshaft Austin racing cars, was also a driver of some skill, and when he first joined the Austin staff used to put in some very fast laps at Brooklands. During his association with E.R.A's he concentrated more upon the technical side.

An Anecdote
I asked Uhlenhaut whether he had any ideas about driving in the races himself, but he shook his head.

"That is not my department", he said. "I only drive the cars to test any points that may arise. I enjoy it all right, but I have no desire to set up as a rival to Caracciola!"

I told him the story about the driver at Le Mans who always said his shock-absorbers were too loose, and used to go round tighten-

Far left. Publicity for Donington by H.J. Moser who was reported to be a German spy. He disappeared prior to hostilities in 1939.

Left. Inkwell, ashtray, vesta case, lighter and toast rack.

A poster by P. Vanderhem for the Dutch Spyker Company who were making a 6-cylinder engine as early as 1903. They went out of business in 1925.

35

ing them up, no matter what the previous adjustment. His confreres, learning this, used to slacken them off beforehand, so that when the driver himself had finished, they were just about correct.

Uhlenhaut laughed, and said that in the Grand Prix team there were few individual foibles, and such matters as tyre pressures and shock-absorber adjustments were all settled by the various technical people, after consultation, of course, with the drivers themselves. Copious notes have been prepared about the various circuits, so there is very little guesswork, even on the preliminary laps.

A fast dual motor road in the Grunewald district outside Berlin was the nucleus of the Avus circuit opened in 1921.

I commented upon the low build of this year's Grand Prix Mercedes, and, citing the example of the "flat-iron" Thomas Specials, asked Uhlenhaut if he thought a car could have too low a centre of gravity. I told him how the Thomas Specials, probably the lowest cars ever built, used to hold the road marvellously up to a point, but would then slide suddenly and uncontrollably, with little warning.

"I have heard of the Thomas Specials", said Uhlenhaut, "but I never saw one in action. However, I do not agree that a car can be too low-built. If, as you say, these machines used to slide without warning, it must have been because in those days less was known about suspension systems. Driving our low-built Grand Prix cars, I always know exactly when they want to skid, and so one can correct accordingly." He made an expressive movement with his hands, as one correcting a skid.

It is certainly a fact that one seldom sees one of the modern Grand Prix cars skid through 180 degrees. If it skids at all, it is usually because the driver wants it to skid, and the whole movement is under control.

Some Opinions

"The advantage of our latest type of rear axle, which I believe you call De Dion-type", went on Uhlenhaut, "is that the wheel-track never varies nor do the wheels tilt at all, so that road adhesion is constant. At the same time, the unsprung weight is very low. The self-locking differential, too, is a great help when one gives the engine the gas in getting away from a corner."

I referred to the comments which have been made concerning the fuel used by the Grand Prix Mercedes, whose pungent fumes should be smelt by spectators at Donington to-day.

"I think that there must be a lot of nonsense talked about our fuel", said Uhlenhaut. "It is not really so special, nor are we the only people who use it. I don't say that if you went to the fuel company and said that you wanted some fuel exactly like that used by the Mercedes cars that they would supply it just like that. However, it is not our own special

formula, and, within limits, anyone could obtain it for a racing car."

"Do you agree that there is any object in using fuel of a more or less ordinary type, or, indeed, in racing with cars bearing some resemblance to production models?" I asked.

"No, I do not", Uhlenhaut replied. "The international body has laid down a formula for Grand Prix races and we build our cars to that formula. If we impose on ourselves the limitations that you mention, our whole scope of design would be handicapped, nor would we get the full benefit of research. The object of Grand Prix racing is to produce a car which with certain definitions of weight or engine size, is the fastest that can be built."

"And the expense?", I said.

Uhlenhaut shrugged his shoulders. "If you take part in Grand Prix racing, you must be prepared for expense", he replied. "How else can progress go on?

"When the 1½-litre formula was in vogue, cars like the Grand Prix Delage and the Talbot-Darracq all had roller-bearing crankshafts. Subsequently, it became more usual to fit plain bearings, even on racing cars, such as the E.R.A. Both last year's and this year's Grand Prix Mercedes, however, have roller-bearings once more."

"Do you have any trouble with rollers?", I asked.

Blown or Unblown?

"No, I consider the roller-bearing shaft, with its absence of friction much superior", said Uhlenhaut. "Nor do we find that they wear out, as I believe used to be the case. We use split cages for the rollers, to avoid a built-up crankshaft. Of course, our engines are stripped after every race, and carefully overhauled, but it is very seldom that we have to renew the rollers."

I next asked what were his views about the respective merits of the 3-litre blown and the 4½-litre unblown engines.

Unblown Possibilities, But -

"At present, we have concentrated upon the 3-litre blown type, as Mercedes-Benz have

always upheld the merits of the supercharger", he answered. "So far as I know, our designers have not yet got out a 4½-litre unsupercharged design, as we naturally want to get our present cars right first. We do not entirely reject the possibilities of that type of engine, however, but it means a new angle of approach. Much research would be necessary for us to get equal performance. Still, I would not like to say definitely that one is better than the other."

Finally, I asked Uhlenhaut a "hot one". "Your drivers sometimes seem nowadays to be racing one another. Can they always be relied upon to obey instructions?"

Keeping It Dark !

Uhlenhaut hesitated a moment. Then he said, "Well, perhaps I can tell you, as none of them talk English – except, of course, Seaman, and he is about the most reliable of them all as regards instructions. We were getting a bit worried at Rheims, as they were overstepping the rev. limits. But then we have something in hand, as we have not actually told them what the rev. limit really is! This is rather a difficult subject, as they are the best drivers in the world, and would be quite irreplaceable."

There now! I always thought Grand Prix drivers were such good boys!

QUALITY AND VALUE THE KEYNOTES OF THIS YEAR'S MOTOR SHOW

Taking things all round the 1939 season promises to be a good one for those motorists anticipating a change of car, for undoubtedly the new cars will prove exceptionally good value. The genius of W. O. Bentley has provided a superb example of a luxury car, and so thorough was the original design that the need for revision does not arise. There is no doubt that the twelve-cylinder Lagonda amply justifies its claim to be a super car in comfort, performance, and roadworthiness. At its price, of course, it should be so. Anyone who can afford to pay £1,500 for a car rightly expects it to be equal to the most exacting demands which could be made of a car which

is generally acknowledged to be among the four or five finest cars in the world, Built to an ideal, it has been enthusiastically received not only in the home market, but also abroad, and for the connoisseur buyer there is no doubt that its appeal is difficult to resist.

Citroen Improvements

"No change for change's sake" is the report of the Citroen Company, who are continuing, with detail improvements, their range which comprises the "Twelve", "Light Fifteen" and "Big Fifteen". The main features of design, including front-wheel drive, integral all-steel construction,independent front wheel suspension, torsion bar springing, overhead valve engine, detachable wet cylinder barrels, and gear lever mounted on facia board are common to all models, and it will be remembered that these features were first embodied by Citroen four years ago. New features common to all models include improved gear shift, with the selector locking device controlled by the clutch, and new type "Michelin" wheels and tyres with a wider rim and tyre section.

With the exception of the two "Popular" models, other new features incorporated include a newly-designed radiator shell, an oil indicator fitted in place of a pressure gauge and giving a more positive warning in case of failure by means of a red light, improved shock absorbers, and polished aluminium protectors fitted to the front end of the rear wings.

CURIOSITIES OF EARLY RACING
By R. King-Farlow

An extremely odd race was that organised by *Le Journal* on August 27th, 1899, from Paris to Trouville. This was a handicap open to any form of transport or locomotion. Pedestrians were sent off at 9 p.m. on August 26th, horses left at 3 a.m. the following morning, cyclists at mid-day, motor-cyclists at 1.45 p.m. and cars at 2 o'clock. Aeroplanes, tanks and aerowheels were unhappily not known in those days, and balloons were probably thought to

offer too much temptation to their occupants in the shape of dropping ballast on rivals' heads as they passed below.

Horses eventually occupied first and second places although the handicap was by no means badly calculated. The winning horse, M. Giren's "Mascotte", averaged 8.5 m.p.h.; the best pedestrian 4.9 m.p.h.; the fastest cyclist 19.4 m.p.h.; the first motorcyclist 32.5 m.p.h., and Antony's Mors 35.2 m.p.h.

Undoubtedly the only instance of a race open to cars in which the winner finished "blown" although starting on atmospheric induction.

Tom Thumb and his seven league boots are outclassed by Peugeot in this Pierre Simmar composition.

Gaston de Fonseca's only known automotive work. A designer in Paris, he also owned a fashionable restaurant there at the turn of the century.

Austrian racing scene, a gouache and crayon study of 1908 by Hugo Klein.

HIGH SOCIETY 1898

From the past week's records of magisterial exploitation of automobilists we extract the following:

"Viscount Northland appeared before Mr. Marsham, at Bow Street, in answer to a summons for driving at 10 miles an hour in St. James's Park. The defendant did not dispute the police evidence, but said he was not aware he was going so quickly. A fine of £3 and 2 shillings. Costs were imposed."

An inspired example of the vogue for employing Heads of State to draw public attention to the motor car.

PARIS FASHIONS
1938

The contrast between the great Motor Shows in London and Paris, held this year over the same period, from October 13th-22nd, is always most interesting.

In London one has the most international display of motor vehicles seen anywhere in the world, but on the Continent there are many unorthodox designs rarely seen in this country, while the difference in body styles is marked. From the point of view of the sportsman, as well as of the student of technical design, there were a great many features of interest at the Paris Salon, more, indeed, than in the some what sober and businesslike atmosphere of Earl's Court.

At the French show actual racing cars can be exhibited, not necessarily offered for sale, and Mercedes-Benz actually displayed one of the Grand Prix models, beside its impressive

list of successes. The gay atmosphere of Paris is typified by the difference between the Grand Palais, just off the Champs Elysees, where the Salon is held, and the severely modern Earl's Court building.

The Grand Palais, with its domed glass roof, and its pillars and statues, represents an earlier style of architecture, while internally much attention is paid to the artistic aspect with a new system of lighting and decoration each year. During the day no artificial light is necessary, and this alone gives a gayer aspect to the exhibits. This year, after dark, the illumination was provided by huge tiers of coloured lamps in the form of Chinese lanterns, transforming the scene into one of great beauty.

Artistic Coachwork

The French have always been renowned for artistic coachwork, and on the more expensive models their designers have a free hand, utilising delicate colours and graceful curves with great effect. Drop-head bodies are popular, and in nearly all cases the hoods can be fixed, if desired, in the three-quarter or "de ville" position, leaving the front compartment open.

Several examples of that most luxurious style of bodywork, the genuine coupe-de-ville, were seen, with the rear seats permanently enclosed, and the driving seat open, or covered by a convertible hood on folding arms. Finest of all was a coupe-de-ville by Franay on a Rolls-Royce chassis, a most striking car with subtle, rounded contours for the enclosed rear compartment. Another fine coupe-de-ville on a Rolls-Royce was shown by Binder, and examples of this style were also seen on Packard and Delage chassis.

Delahaye

A centre of attraction on the Delahaye stand was the magnificent drop-head roadster body on the 4½-litre twelve-cylinder car, with chassis similar to that of the Grand Prix models. All the wheels were fully enclosed by fairings, and the lamps were also sunk into the streamlining in a most unobtrusive manner. This car had a Cotal magnetic gearbox, and a single downdraught Solex carburettor, in place of the three fitted on the racing cars. In France, with the favourable rate of exchange now prevailing, the chassis price is 138,000 francs, or less than £800.

There is also a new 3½-litre six-cylinder Delahaye engine, with the same bore and stroke as before, but with modifications to the block and head on the lines of the Grand Prix engine.

Peugeot now confine their range to two models, the new "292", with 1,133 c.c. engine, independent front suspension by torsion bars, and a petrol consumption of 40-45 m.p.g., and the "402", of just over 2-litres capacity. This latter model is also available as the 402 Legere, with a shorter wheelbase, and it was a car of this type which was so successful at Le Mans in 1937 and 1938. A very useful looking sports model was shown, with two-seater body, and fully enclosed rear wheels.

The "202" model illustrates one of the main tendencies evident at the Salon, for more economical motoring, just as at Earl's Court. French manufacturers have been affected, to an even greater degree than their British *confreres*, by recent international affairs, and are paying such attention to good petrol consumption, especially since fuel in France is considerably more expensive than in this country, owing to a high tax.

The small Citroen, about which rumours have been circulating for some time, has not yet appeared, but there was a new "legere" six-cylinder Citroen at the Salon, with an engine of nearly 3-litres in the front-wheel-drive chassis also used for the 2-litre car, and it should thus have an excellent performance.

La Licorne

The French have always specialised in small sports cars, which in the past have sometimes seemed a little spidery to English eyes. Several of these have now grown up, and the new La Licorne is vastly improved. It has an interesting frame in the form of a double Y. The engine is held in the front fork, and the

41

frame is then swept in to form a short, central backbone, before sweeping out to each end of the rear axle.

The engine is mounted as far forward as possible in the chassis, and the independent front suspension is by semi-cantilever springs, placed at an oblique angle to the frame. There are two engine sizes, one of 1,100 c.c., and the other just over 1½-litres. The former has a four-speed gearbox, and the latter three speeds, the price being the same.

A front-wheel-drive sports machine is the Georges Irat, which has also made a big technical advance. The new models have a frame in the form of a U, with the engine mounted between the open arms at the front. In this case all four wheels are independently sprung, by a system of rubber rings, which also incorporate a shock-absorbing effect. The gear lever is conveniently mounted on the dashboard. The smaller model has an 1,100 c.c. Ruby engine, and the bigger Georges Irat, an entirely new model, has the 2-litre Citroen unit. Yet another 1,100 c.c. sports car is the Danvignes again with independent suspension of all four wheels.

Bugatti has such reputation that he can afford to disregard such trifles as independent suspension, and his cars – it is strange how Bugatti is always singular, whereas other makes are plural – preserve their traditional lines, though more luxurious than of yore. His Stelvio Cabriolet, finished in two delicate shades of green, and with the headlamps streamlined into the wing fairings, was one of the best-lookers in a Show remarkable for fine cars.

Talbot-Darracq had sent their competition two-seater, Lago Special to London, but had several of these 4-litre models with fine cabriolet and saloon bodies on view. With touring coachwork, these cars are reputed to attain about 105 m.p.h., while the two-seater is said to reach 115 m.p.h. Wilson-type pre-selector gearboxes are fitted. A new four-cylinder 2.3-litre Talbot-Darracq appeared at the Salon, with an ordinary type of gearbox, which can also be fitted on the larger models at option.

There were many fine Delages, both on the firm's own stand and among the specialist coachbuilders, whose exhibits were in a gallery at the side of the main hall, unfortunately not so well lighted as the rest of the Grand Palais. One splendid example of a drop-head foursome body on the "D8-120" chassis attracted much admiration.

Drop-head Bodies

French coachbuilders have mastered the art of constructing the hood on a drop-head body in such a manner that it can be folded away right out of sight, thus giving an even neater appearance than that of an open touring car. This is a point worthy of much attention, for it seems inevitable that this latter type will in the end be replaced by the convertible body, except for purely sporting purposes.

British exhibits at the Salon were this year confined to Rolls-Royce Bentley, Humber, and Hillman, and apart from French coachwork of exceptionally luxurious type on the former two makes, were the same as the examples seen at Earl's Court. When one considers that there were sixty-five different makes of car at the London Show, it is remarkable that in Paris, out of about fifty different types exhibited, nearly a score were peculiar to the French exhibition.

An 1894 poster and arguably the earliest surviving one. The make survived until 1901, turning out some 50 cars.

The 1938 Swiss Grand Prix won by Caracciola. The Englishman, Dick Seaman, was placed second.

La route vous sourit avec...

ENERGOL

EN VENTE ICI

Energol 1930 by Réné Vincent, equally at home with fashion or cars.

43

"The Challenge Cup" awarded for the Austrain Alpine Rallies 1912-1914. Klinkosch, the crown jeweller, here depicts the gods of Earth, Wind and Fire looking down on an Audi touring car designed by Ferdinand Porsche.

MECHANIZED GERMANY ON PARADE
1939

When Germany has a Motor Show, there is no possibility of anyone in Berlin overlooking the fact. There is just that same showmanship which lends to a Grand Prix race the glamour so often lacking for an event in England. During the period of the Earl's Court show, a chance visitor to London, not interested in motor cars, might notice merely that there was more traffic than usual, and that the hotels were unusually full.

Had such a visitor been in Berlin on February 17th, he would have been awakened early in the morning by the roar of racing cars, with open exhausts, assembling outside the Chancellory. The great new road, with twin carriage ways, which is being built right through Berlin, was lined for six or seven miles by thousands of uniformed N.S.K.K. troopers, all the way from the Unter den Linden and the Brandenburg Tor right through the Tiergarten – Germany's Hyde Park – and along the spacious Kaiserdamm road to Charlottenburg, where the nine exhibition halls are situated on the outskirts of the city, close to the Avus track.

Opening Ceremonial

Behind the lines of troopers, thousands upon thousands of spectators were waiting to catch a glimpse of the Fuhrer as he drove in state to perform the opening ceremony. The Mercedes-Benz and Auto-Union Grand Prix cars headed the procession, together with the B.M.W. sports cars and the racing motor cycles which have won so many laurels during the past season. Herr Hitler's Grosser Mercedes touring car was followed by other resplendent vehicles, filled with uniformed Cabinet ministers and officials. The splendid

procession was like a State opening of Parliament.

Huge blood-red banners dropped from the walls of the exhibition buildings, with the Nazi swastika flaring on all sides. Inside the first hall hundreds of chairs faced a raised dais from which the Fuhrer was to deliver his opening speech. On either side of the dais the two models of the new Volkswagen, or People's Car, were proudly displayed, backed by huge crimson velvet curtains which veiled the exhibition proper.

Herr Hitler said that cars were no longer a luxury, but had become an article of daily use. Prices had been adjusted to bring motoring within the reach of all classes of the people, and his aim was to have not only the densest but also the safest traffic in Europe. The addition of new areas to the Reich had opened up an even greater market than hitherto. The demand for cars, he said, was unlimited, and he had made arrangements to satisfy it.

He announced, too, that it was the will of the Government that car radio should be improved and brought within the purchasing powers of all. Faced by this order, the industry will have to buckle to, just as they have done in the case of the People's Car.

The number of types of German cars, said Herr Hitler, was to be drastically reduced, in order that production should be upon the most economical basis.

After a severe warning to reckless drivers, to whom he referred as "vermin", robbing the nation in six years of as many people as were killed in the whole of the Franco-Prussian war, Herr Hitler declared the exhibition open, the velvet curtains were rolled back, and the Fuhrer, accompanied by Reichsminister Goebbels and Field-Marshal Goering, began a tour of the exhibits, which included not only cars but motor cycles, commercial vehicles, radio sets, accessories, synthetic materials, and special vehicles used by the Post Office and the Army. Amongst the latter was a huge 30-ton tank, a startling vehicle.

Yet with all this spectacle, the vast Berlin Motor Show does not compare with that at Earl's Court as an exhibition of the world's motor vehicles. Whereas the Earl's Court show is the most international in the world, the Berlin *Ausstellung* a rampant display of German nationalism. It is Germany's mechanized programme on parade. There were a few British, French Italian, and American cars, but the bulk of the exhibits was from the home country.

Big things have been happening in the German motor industry during the past year. As part of the drive to capture the world's markets – in which the programme of Grand Prix racing plays an important part – a special State official, Colonel von Schell, has been appointed to organize production. He has already put into force a schedule reducing the number of types of commercial vehicles, and during the coming year the same limitation will be enforced upon car manufacturers. Already no firm may produce a new model between 2-litres and 3½-litres without permission from the Government.

Marking Time

Thus at present, as might be expected, there is a tendency for the industry to mark time, though it may be noted that even marking time is not a sedentary occupation.

Secondly, the production of the People's

The 1938 German Grand Prix was won by Seaman driving a Mercedes W154. He married Erika Popp, daughter of the BMW Chairman and was to lose his life at Spa the following year.

Hans Liska was responsible for this 1939 Tripoli poster.

Car cannot fail to have a marked effect upon the industry in general. This machine has been awaited for several years, and even now is not on the market, though the design is fixed, and the German people has for some time been subscribing towards future purchase.

A scheme has been got out-by which a card is obtained to be gradually filled with 5 Rm. stamps, towards the total cost of 995 Rm. In English money this is equivalent to about £65, though an exact computation is difficult owing to the varying methods of calculating the exchange. It is said that 1,000,000 Rm. per week is being subscribed in this manner, while 170,000 People's Cars have already been ordered and paid for, though deliveries will not begin until early next year.

State Assistance

The purchase price of the People's Car is small indeed, but one must not forget that it is to be manufactured under the direct control of the State, and that the special company responsible has no selling and advertising costs, with a guaranteed market, has no necessity to show a profit for shareholders, nor is there any discount for agents. Raw materials, too, are supplied by the State at the most favourable rates. Granted all these advantages, there seems little question that several British manufacturers could cut the price of existing models to an equivalent rate, if such a procedure were considered desirable, which is open to doubt.

In Germany, the People's Car is now generally known as the "K. d. F. Wagen", or "Strength through Joy" car. There are two body styles, of similar design except that one has a fixed roof, while the other has a folding top of flexible material. Both seat four people, with a tolerable amount of leg room.

All four wheels are independently sprung, by means of torsion bars. The 986 c.c. air-cooled engine has four horizontally opposed cylinders, and is placed at the rear, securing its cooling by means of a large blower or fan. Luggage space is provided, both behind the rear seat, and in front under the "bonnet." The headlamps are set in the wings, and the body is quite well streamlined, so that some 60 m.p.h. and 40 m.p.g. are said to be possible.

The nearest competitor to the People's Car in Germany is the Opel Cadet, which costs approximately twice the price. This car shows no appreciable alteration this year, but in the Opel range there is one new model, the 2½-litre six-cylinder Captain, which has a form of integral construction, the steel body shell being used to reinforce the chassis, as on the smaller model. Independent front suspension by coil springs is used.

Auto-Union

Another small car which has proved very

The most famous mascot of them all, the Spirit of Ectasy created by Charles Sykes, R.A.

Original artwork by
Rene Roussel.

popular in Germany is the small two-stroke Auto-Union D.K.W., which has a new box-section frame, built to allow a low floor level. Of the other members of the Auto-Union combine, Wanderer continued their existing models, and the most striking newcomers at the Berlin Show were the 3.2-litre six-cylinder Audi, with front wheel drive, and the 3.8-litre V8 Horch. The former car was a real good-looker, with a fine power to weight ratio of 48 lbs. per h.p. A maximum speed of 80 m.p.h., and a cruising speed of 73 m.p.h., is claimed.

The new Horch is an improvement upon the former 3.5-litre V8, and the engine now develops 92 h.p. One of the models exhibited had a super-streamlined body equipped for long-distance touring, with seats folding flat to form a couch, and a wash-basin, with hot and cold water laid on, folding into one of the front wings. The big 5-litre straight-eight Horch is also continued.

Pride of place on the Mercedes-Benz stand must be given to the sporting and beautifully designed roadster built for Korpfuhrer Huhnlein, leader of the N.S.K.K., who recently averaged over 80 m.p.h. with it from the middle of Berlin to Munich, a distance of more than 600 miles. This car was not actually in the production range, being a development of the 5.4-litre supercharged model, with a 5.8-litre engine and a shorter and lighter chassis. It is said to have a maximum speed of over 140 m.p.h. It also has a five-speed gearbox, and this feature is the main alteration in the 5.4-litre standard model, apart from larger and improved shock-absorbers. The geared-up top ratio of 2.8 to 1 gives a speed of 90 m.p.h. at 2,700 r.p.m., a speed which, it is said, can be maintained without using the supercharger.

Other Mercedes Models

Of the other Mercedes models on view, the most interesting new development was the adoption of the X-type oval tube frame, as used on the 1.7-litre model, for the 2.3-litre car also. The 2.3-litre has a larger fuel tank, and a quick adjustment for the distributor to enable the engine to be run on various types of fuel, according to the anti-knock value.

All-steel bodies of a new type have been designed for the 2.3-litre car, with a forward

radiator mounting and a bonnet opening at the top, with a catch operated from inside the car.

The engine size of the Type 320 Mercedes has been increased from 3.2-litres to 3.4-litres, but in order to meet the requirements of lower octane fuel, the compression ratio has been lowered, so that the power output is about the same as before. This model is specially designed for fast cruising speeds on the *autobahnenn*, and has an overdrive which permits the maximum speed of the car, some 80 m.p.h., to be used continuously.

In the Hall of Honour, the streamlined Mercedes racing car, fresh from its exploits at Dessau, was shown, as well as the older 5½-litre model which Caracciola used last spring in attaining 268 m.p.h., and the now familiar 3-litre road-racing car. Auto-Union showed their super-streamlined car which holds the world's standing start mile and kilometre records, and also a Grand Prix model. The B.M.W. sports car and the Hanomag-Diesel record-car also received a place in the Hall of Honour, where the central exhibit was a stripped chassis of the People's Car.

In the main hall one of the finest streamlined bodies was that on the Tatra, with 3-litre air-cooled V8 engine at the rear. The Tatra was formerly a Czecho-Slovakian make, but since the works are at Nesseldorf, in Sudetenland, it now ranks as German, in the same way that the Steyr, formerly Austrian, is now also German. The Czech motor industry still had the Skoda and the Praga Piccolo in the

show. Both have engines of 1,100 c.c. and have all four wheels independently sprung.

Streamlining has always been a feature of Adler cars, designed for high cruising speeds. The striking 2.5-litre car is said to have a maximum of nearly 90 m.p.h. B.M.W. did not show their super-streamlined saloon again, and interest centred on the new 3.5-litre model, seen at Earl's Court, with its fine power to weight ratio, and the sports two-seater T.T. model.

It was a disappointment not to see the new 2-litre supercharged Hansa at the *Ausstellung*, for phenomenal speeds are claimed for it, and the specification, with tubular backbone chassis and all-independent suspension, is very striking. The Hansa is now known as the Borgward, following a reconstruction of the company, and the other models of 1,100 c.c., 2-litres, and 3½-litres, were exhibited under this name.

A new German car is the 1.3-litre Hanomag, interesting because it is one of the only new small cars in the show, through the shadow of the impending Volkswagen. The Hanomag has independent front suspension by means of rubber in torsion.

From Other Countries

The Italian cars in the show were Lancia and Alfa-Romeo, Renault and Bugatti came from France, and Hudson from the U.S.A. Great Britain was represented by Humber, Hillman, and Sunbeam-Talbot, some of the models having German-built cabriolet bodies, and by Austin, while a Rolls-Royce was seen on one of the special coachwork stands.

There were special exhibits of synthetic materials, such as Plexiglass which has only half the weight of ordinary glass, and the Buhre artificial rubber, whose cost has now been much reduced. It is stated that during the present year tyres of Buhre rubber will be used on all German cars. The light metal industry also had a number of exhibits. From a technical point of view the Berlin show is always full of interest, but its main feature is that it is the showroom of the national policy of mechanization.

Maurice Roussillon (the artist O'Galop) devised the successful Michelin Man, alias Bibendum.

The entry of Mercedes (seen here) and Auto-Union "silver torpedoes" enlivened Grand Prix racing in the second half of the thirties.

The Georges Irat. more sporting in appearance than in performance, was produced until 1939.

THE ASTON MARTIN SPEED MODEL
1939

My intention was to test the 15/98 short chassis tourer but when I arrived at the Aston-Martin works, and saw the recently introduced streamline Speed Model, I naturally wished to try this instead.

The car was just as it had come in and it had not been touched for 2,000 miles, but the makers sportingly allowed me to take it away. It was raining a little and there was such a high wind that the training planes at Hanworth Aerodrome, which adjoins the works, were grounded. I would have preferred to wait for a more favourable day, but circumstances would not permit it.

This model is frankly a racing car planned for club events. It will be hand-built in limited quantities at £775.

Viewed from the top the car is of pear-drop shape, the widest part being the bonnet just in front of the dash this form offering the least head resistance.

Designed for Speed

In these days when so many sports cars are merely standard touring vehicles fitted with special bodywork, higher gear ratios and a high-compression cylinder head, it is a real joy to examine a machine designed from the ground up for sheer speed and all the thrills that go with it.

The engine has an overhead camshaft and a special hollow Nitralloy hardened crankshaft. Nitralloy, by the way, gives the hardest surface known to engineering. The special high-compression head has polished ports and it is used in conjunction with two S.U. carburettors and a welded-up exhaust system in which each cylinder has its own outlet pipe. Racing timing is used, and the lubrication is on the dry sump system.

Belts being considered unreliable at elevated speeds the dynamo is positively driven from the engine. Devoid of such concessions to the inexpert as a synchro-mesh the gearbox is of the four-speed racing type, which really does provide a lightning change.

GROSSER PREIS DER SCHWEIZ FÜR AUTOMOBIL BERN 26. AUGUS 193

This powerful and dynamic composition was created for the first Swiss Grand Prix by the illustrator Kaspar Ernst Graf.

Oil on board artwork for Dunlop shows St. James's Palace by C.E. Turner.

St. James's Palace, London

51

One could go on writing pages and pages on the clever design of this fascinating machine, but sufficient has been noted to make it clear that this model must not be judged by ordinary standards. It is an out and out speed automobile.

The first thing that impressed itself winding in and out among the traffic was the ease and rapidity of the gear change. Up, it is a rapid flick of the wrist. Down, a couple of dabs of the clutch pedal and a moment of the accelerator in between, as you push the lever through the gate. I made many unnecessary changes for the sheer joy of playing with that short, rigid control. Some of the up and down changes from top to third were made at "seventy per".

The next thing that impresses one when handling a car of this kind, built by a firm of Aston-Martin's racing experience, is its supreme safety and responsiveness. When you put your foot down, while travelling in one of the lower gears, the response is thrilling and immediate. When you turn the steering wheel the car turns as accurately as if it were running on rails. You feel that you can place the model exactly where you like, when you like and how you like. It is an inspiring machine to handle. And the brakes … but more of these later.

Both the speedometer and the rev. indicator are chronometric, their hands moving with the purposeful motion of their kind. The instruments proved to as accurate as it is possible to make them, the speedometer being dead right at 30, .7 m.p.h. fast at 40, .55 fast at 50, and .79 m.p.h. fast at 60. In each case the engine speed indicator was found to be dead accurate for the engine speeds matched up with the speedometer readings according to specification. The safe maximum is 5,500 r.p.m., which equals 41 m.p.h. in bottom, 56 in second gear and 76 m.p.h. in third. It was impossible to reach 5,500 in top.

Unfortunately, the full Brooklands lap is still unavailable, for, although the track repairs have been completed, men are still working near the Fork on the extension to the Vickers factory. A couple of bombers were also being erected on the track at the Fork.

Speed Tests
The wind was roaring up the Railway Straight with such force that the best speed that I could obtain with the main screen down and one aero screen erected was 88.24 m.p.h. I have no doubt that, under favourable conditions, speeds in the region of 100 m.p.h. could be

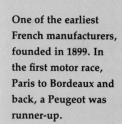

obtained with full road equipment.

As was to be expected the acceleration was impressive. From 10 to 30 m.p.h. took 3.2 secs. in bottom gear, 5.0 secs. in second, and 7.8 secs. in third. No top gear times were attempted because nice people do not drive racing cars at 10 m.p.h. on a 4.4 to 1 top ratio.

Rest to 50 required but one gear change. Bottom gear was held until the speedometer needle came up to near the 40 mark and then third was engaged. It took 9 seconds. Standstill to 60 was performed in the lower three gears, the third being engaged at 55. In three successive tests the time was 14.0 secs.

Superlative Braking
Aston-Martin brakes have always been excellent, but the new anchors fitted to this model are decidedly super. The ribbed brake-drums are as large as can be accommodated within

One of the earliest French manufacturers, founded in 1899. In the first motor race, Paris to Bordeaux and back, a Peugeot was runner-up.

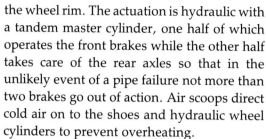

the wheel rim. The actuation is hydraulic with a tandem master cylinder, one half of which operates the front brakes while the other half takes care of the rear axles so that in the unlikely event of a pipe failure not more than two brakes go out of action. Air scoops direct cold air on to the shoes and hydraulic wheel cylinders to prevent overheating.

The patented torque reaction system used on the front axle holds the castor angle constant through the medium of a steel cable when the brakes are applied. Hence the car is extremely stable under severe braking and it always comes to rest in a straight line. In three successive tests it stopped in 27 feet from 30 m.p.h. In one of them it stopped in a straight line hands off the steering wheel.

As should be on a model of this kind, the steering is high geared, only 2⅛th turns of the wheel being necessary to swing the car from one full lock to the other. The column is adjustable for rake so that it is possible to position the wheel sufficiently low to see over it.

I always think that the supreme tests for steering is to drive round the banking hands off and, if the car holds its correct position on the banking, according to its speed, then all is well. This auto passed the test handsomely on the Byfleet Banking for more than half-a-mile at 80 m.p.h.

In my usual trials on the Test Hill I found that the racing type hand brake which, by the way, is ideally positioned, would hold the car on the 1 in 4, but, while the model would just get away from a standstill on this grade, the 11.38 to 1 bottom gear is really too high for such a manoeuvre to be executed in comfort. (The standard Aston-Martin bottom gear is 16.8 to 1.) I do not hold this against the car, for stop-and-restart tests on freak gradients do not come within the province of a racing car and, if the bottom gear were lowered, the standing start acceleration on more usually encountered gradients, or the flat, would suffer.

In all normal running the water temperature fluctuated between 75 and 90 degrees, but repeated acceleration tests on the

lower two gears and on the Test Hill did cause a little boiling.

The car is brimful of clever features. The screen, for instance, has a centre hinge in addition to the two side hinges which have positive locks for the up and down positions. Wind deflectors are fitted to the sides of the main screen which form aero screens when the main screen is folded flat. Very light and simple to erect is the hood. A tubular steel bow is plugged into sockets behind the seat and over this the hood cover is laid, being attached to the screen by a pair of thumb-screws and to the body by seven "press-the-

dot" fasteners.

Under the bonnet the layout is workman-like. Opening the near-side half of the bonnet shows that the carburettors, electric petrol pumps, magneto, dynamo and battery are all accessible. On the off side is the exhaust pipe and sparking plugs, the wide sweeping pipes being sufficiently far from the plugs to allow of comfortable working. The removal of three nuts suffices to release the valve cover to reach the valve adjusters. A special cup is included in the tool-kit which can be bolted to the front of the camshaft chain wheel when the camshaft is uncoupled. The cup attaches the wheel to a bracket on the cylinder block which prevents the timing being lost.

The body is adequately wide, measuring 3ft. 6ins. inside at the instrument panel. A small luggage locker, sufficiently large for a coat and a couple of attache cases, is provided in the tail. There is room for a further small amount of luggage in the spare wheel locker so that the clubman and his passenger can travel to the venue with such spare clothing as they may require. Under the bonnet there is a commodious felt-lined container for tools and spares. This newcomer will definitely uphold its makers' high reputation.

IN THE PEOPLE'S CAR
By Patrick Wynn

On the way to Dessau I was able to travel in one of the new People's Cars. Unfortunately, no instructions had been given that anyone else besides the works driver should handle the car, and, you know, in Germany nothing can be done without instructions. It transpired later that, apart from the works testers, only Korpsfuhrer Huhnlein, leader of Germany motor sport, *and one other* had driven the People's Car. I must say I was intrigued to know who the *one other* was, but this apparently could not be stated.

Thus I can only give my impressions from the passenger's seat but these may be interesting to readers, even if the Volkswagen is not in general their type of meat. It certainly seemed a workmanlike little car, even if when one tapped the roof from the inside it gave a hollow ring rather like a bath! The speedometer was a little fast, but the car proved capable of its claimed 60 m.p.h., and

held a speed of between 55 and 60 m.p.h. for many miles along the *autobahn* without apparently tiring.

The engine showed plenty of acceleration, considering its small size, but the gears, at any rate on the car in which I was driven, were extremely noisy, and sounded rather as though one had engaged a supercharger, though naturally the same effect was not forthcoming. Sitting in the back seat, too, one was at first somewhat conscious of noise from the engine, just behind, but this soon wore off – the consciousness of noise, not the engine.

There was not quite as much legroom as I had been led to expect, but on the other hand the head-room was excellent, and it was quite possible to sit upright, wearing a felt hat, in the back seat without any fear of bumping one's head on the roof, and producing the bath-like note. Head-room is not a feature which all modern cars possess, especially those with sloping, streamlined tails, like that of the Volkswagen.

The suspension and cornering appeared to

The most popular metal used by the European artists of the day was bronze. Works produced repeatedly show a commendable degree of technical mastery.

"The Motorists" by Heinz Muller who studied at the Academy of Dusseldorf details motoring attire of the day. Germany c.1912. Bronze 9½" × 3⅝".

be excellent, though the former was a little harsh at low speeds, and the brakes also were, so it seemed, of fully adequate power. As a minor point, I was impressed by the provision of twin screen-wipers, an unusual feature of a small, cut-price car. The external finish of the body and engine were also surprisingly good, though this particular car was not, of course, a production model, but one of the many built for testing purposes.

Passing from the world's cheapest car to one of the most expensive, I was privileged to return from Berlin with Pomeroy, jun., of *The Motor*, in a 12-cylinder Lagonda, a car in which one could really settle down to enjoy an *autobahn*. We were not out for any long distance records but the car seemed to be going so well that not to tabulate its performance would be a crime.

We had at our disposal some 215 miles of *autobahn*, from the beginning of the Ring Road round Berlin, so far as this has yet been completed, to a point west of Hanover. For the first quarter of an hour Pomeroy averaged

no fewer than 100.6 m.p.h., and, with the traffic steadily increasing managed to cover 156.6 kilometres in one hour, an average of 97.24 m.p.h., without ever having the car flat out. I know that this was the case, because I was watching the rev. counter, and subsequently drove the car myself.

The Hanover *autobahn* will in a short time connect up with another stretch running from the great industrial areas round Cologne, Essen, Dusseldorf, and Dortmund, and as we got farther west the traffic grew steadily worse. It was extremely noticeable this year that traffic on the *autobahnen* is much thicker, and one meets in particular many more commercial vehicles of gigantic size, thundering along, and taking an immense time to pass one another.

The German method of driving on the *autobahnen* is most trying to anyone in a fast car. They swing out to pass another vehicle sometimes 100 yards before they reach it, and allow an equally long distance to pass before they pull in again. A total width of 32 feet is

The start of the 1938 German Grand Prix. Mercedes and Auto-Union were invincible in the expert hands of Rosemeyer, Caracciola, Nuvolari and others.

inadequate for such methods, for I have never seen a case in which three cars could, pass one another abreast, though with all the traffic on either side of the *autobahn* going in the same direction, this would be perfectly safe. When all the Volkswagens get going, I should say that fast averages on an *autobahn* would be almost impossible.

A Fine Performance

Well, to return to the Lagonda, as traffic grew thicker during the second hour, our average began to drop, but for our last quarter-hour period, things improved, and, though we were baulked twice by lorries, the average again topped the three figure mark, at 100.1 m.p.h., while the total average for the two hours was no less than 91.29 m.p.h. I should mention that during this second hour we stopped to fill up with petrol, otherwise we should have had the stupendous average of over 95 m.p.h. Beat that, some of you average speed merchants!

The fastest speed recorded during the run was 105 m.p.h. for two kilometres. Shortly after the two hours mark, we entered a stretch of road under construction, and had to slow up a lot, but for the whole 215 miles averaged 87 m.p.h. After that we ran out of *autobahn*.

Giuseppe Riccobaldi's original dated "Anno VII", in common with all Italian posters produced whilst Mussolini was in power and denoting the 7th year of his reign.

A BAD CASE
1905

Sir — "Garage Proprietor", who wrote in your last issue, was quite right to prevent a careless chauffeur endangering his property and that of other people. But if it had been on my promises I should have kicked the insolent fool out, and not waited for him to go.

"Another Garage Owner"

SHOULD MOTOR-MEN HAVE HOLIDAYS?
1905

Sir — Will you tell me if you consider that a chauffeur is entitled to an annual holiday? To me it seems that here, at any rate, is a trade where such a privilege should not be allowed to become one of the ever-increasing "rights" of those who serve us. The primary object of a holiday, I take it, is to afford the tired town-worker a short period of rest, and fresh air, and change of scenery and surroundings, and to such the annual holiday is a just and beneficent institution. I cannot but think, however, that a motor-man comes under another category altogether. My man's life seems to me to be one continual round of enjoyment. Touring all through the summer months supplies him with all the fresh air and change of scenery he may require; during the winter, beyond a month or six weeks on the Riviera the car goes out but little, and he is then able to enjoy whatever rest may be necessary.

I have to supply my chauffeur with a singularly good and reliable car, and year out

year in beyond the ordinary routine work (petrol, oil, grease, water, etc.) his duties are limited to mending an occasional puncture, all washing, polishing, etc. being done in the garage and charged in the bill; for this I pay him £3 per week and his expenses when away from London. And yet he asked me this morning when it would be convenient that he should take "his holiday".

Now, sir, I have no wish to appear a hard task-master or to contravene any custom, but do you not think that this is asking too much?

Costumes And Chatter
1905

My Dear Diana — The Christmas bazaars are in swing and the Christmas numbers are out.

Yuletide gifts stare us in the face, and, as usual, it is a case of *embarrassement de richess* in the choice of souvenirs to bestow on our dearest friends.

Motorist's *pot pourri* would be a good Christmas present, don't you think? Naturally the perfume would require renewing somewhat often, for it is hardly to be expected that a delicate scent could long withstand the violent currents of air to which it would be subjected under the expressed conditions.

Motor foot-warmers, labelled as the cosiest of yuletide gifts, are other worthy objects displayed, together with handsome fur motor-sacks, and when once you are tucked inside one of these, Diana, you are rendered practically invulnerable to chill and can laugh at the frost.

MONACO
8 AOUT 1937

Monaco Publicity 1937
a lithograph by
Geo Ham.

DRIVERS ALL

Glimpses in a gallery:

some outstanding figures

from the golden years

George Eyston tamed the difficult Panhard at the banked Montlhèry circuit near Paris.

Tripoli, the fastest of all road circuits. In the 1938 Grand Prix the "Mercs" triumphed 1, 2, 3.

MRS. HAWKES LOOKS BACK
By Dennis May 1938

In this era of ballyhoo it is refreshing to meet a celebrity to whom personal publicity means precisely nothing. "You would have to depart considerably from the truth in order to make an interesting article out of my record-breaking experiences, and this I am very much averse to your doing." Thus Mrs. Gwenda Hawkes, when I wrote to her suggesting that she might be willing to be interviewed.

Records

Well, that might be her opinion, but after all Mrs. Hawkes does hold the Montlhèry lap record, irrespective of sex, at 147.2 m.p.h., and the Women's Record for the Brooklands outer circuit at 135.95 m.p.h.; she has travelled faster on four wheels than any other member of her sex, and faster in a three-wheeler than any living person. Few drivers, furthermore, share with her the distinction of having crashed while travelling at over 150 m.p.h. and lived to tell the tale – reluctantly."

If these experiences failed to provide material for an interesting article, the time had obviously come for the interviewer to take a correspondence course in interviewing.

Racing drivers who made their first acquaintance with the century on two wheels not uncommonly attribute to motor cycle experience much of the success they afterwards achieve. Mrs. Hawkes is an exception. Ex-motor cyclist readers will probably remember her feats at the track on a big twin Triumph machine in the early "twenties".

"Motor cycle racing is good fun", she said, "but in my particular case I doubt whether the experience was of much subsequent value. Motor cyclists, you know, often make rotten car drivers. Three-wheelers probably taught me more than anything else about handling a car like the Derby, which, of course, is very light for its speed. Although entirely different in general layout, a Morgan has a lot in common with a Derby, so far as high-speed navigation is concerned. Both handle beauti-

fully, but they strongly resent the use of brute force on the wheel if and when difficulties arise."

A ruefully reminiscent smile crossed Mrs. Hawkes's face when I asked her what it feels like to average 115.66 m.p.h. "both ways" in a three-wheeler, weighing only 6 cwts., on the narrow and steeply-cambered Arpajon stretch.

Nightmare Ride

"That, I don't mind telling you, was a nightmare ride", she said. "On sand or salt it would have been easy, but if the choice of course is limited to Arpajon it's no wonder our record has stood for eight years.

"It is an actual fact", Mrs. Hawkes went on, "that we should never have got the record – or at least, not at anything like 115 – if I hadn't been in such a state of terror. Our Morgan, like a standard job, had a motor cycle-type throttle lever on a spoke of the steering wheel, instead of a pedal. And to prevent it vibrating shut we had given the lever a stiff setting before starting out.

"When the speed got up to about 110 m.p.h., the machine simply did what it pleased – leapt from one verge to the other like a bronco. I would have given anything I possessed to able to shut off, but just didn't dare take a hand off the wheel rim to reach the throttle. I remember noticing, out of the corner of my eye, how the two lines of spectators were retiring to a safe distance – and envying them the ability to go where they wanted.

The Return Trip

"When the timekeepers told me my speed for the one-way run – well above the existing record – there was really no choice but to 'be a man' and tackle the return trip, funk or no funk. Anyhow, I knew by that time that the machine could be kept right side up even if it did travel about three-quarters of a mile between the so-called kilometre lines."

"Which do you consider the least difficult", I asked, "lapping Montlhèry or Brooklands at 135 m.p.h.?"

EARL HOWE

HON. BRIAN LEWIS

"Personally", replied Mrs. Hawkes. "I find Montlhèry the easier proposition, but probably that is only because I happen to know the Autodrome better than Brooklands. Familiarity is everything. I'd turned Brooklands at over 130 only about half a dozen times in my life, when the existing Women's Lap Record was set up, whereas Montlhèry is home from home to me.

"The snag at Brooklands, as everyone knows, is the unbanked and completely blind curve made by the Vickers factory. A front-wheel-drive car like the Derby is delightfully tractable, but as I said just now, one mustn't attempt to point it somewhere it doesn't want to go. The Big Bump over the Wey Viaduct is another potential snare for a light machine. First time round at really high speed I took the Derby over the Bump and although I lifted my foot for the whoopsy-daisy, just as it tells you in the first primers, the whole transmission was smashed on landing.

"Subsequently, I have always steered a course below the Bump. If the Bump occurred

at any other point on the Circuit this would be impossible, but here one has the whole length and breadth of the Railway Straight in which to rectify any untoward results of the swoop."

Brooklands Lap Record

I put in: "What about the lap record? It seems conceivable that the 2-litre Derby could be made to go round the outer circuit faster than anything yet."

"Yes, I think so too", Mrs. Hawkes concurred, "although John Cobb doesn't agree with me. Of course, he is quite right when he says that the Napier Railton can be eased off to, say, 130 m.p.h. at the tricky spots and still average 143.44 m.p.h. for the whole trip; whereas the Derby would have to be held practically flat the whole way. It would be interesting to try it, although it's not likely that I shall have the chance, as both the Derbys are for sale. Racing and record-

breaking simply doesn't pay us these days, and as you see, we have plenty to keep us busy here."

This last remark was accompanied by a gesture which embraced the premises and effects of the Brooklands Engineering Company, Limited, of which enterprise Mr. and Mrs. Hawkes are principals. A buzz of industry from the workshop, adjacent to the office in which we sat, confirmed the words.

150 m.p.h. at Montlhèry

The conversation next turned to Montlhèry, a piste I never visit without marvelling at the courage of anyone who laps it at close on 150 m.p.h. Montlhèry, of course, is completely unlike Brooklands, being symmetrically formed of two equal and parallel straights, and a pair of corresponding curves, banked a good deal more steeply than the Weybridge concrete. The bankings, moreover, are artificially

French Shell poster of the inter-war years. "That's Shell that was!" was one of the most famous slogans of its day for the home market.

The San Sebastian circuit in the Basque region of Northern Spain was introduced in 1923.

raised on piles, so that over the top there is nothing but thin air and a long drop. Around each lip a fence runs, with ominous looking gaps at intervals. The fences couldn't hope to stop a car, if it once went utterly berserk, but it has always seemed to me that those gaps would exert an unmanning influence on anyone engaged in Mrs. Hawkes's hobby of "being a man".

A Difficult Track

"Yes, I used to find the gaps disconcerting", she admitted. "They took my mind off the rather serious business of placing the car correctly at the start of the bankings, so I got the track authorities to paint a black line on the concrete at the entrance to each turn. The main purpose of the lines was to act as a mark at which to aim the offside front wheel, but they also diverted one's attention from those gaps and the void beyond. Later, it was suggested by a visiting English driver – I forget who – that a black line should be painted round the full periphery of the Autodrome, and those who knew no better hailed this as a stroke of genius. Actually, of course, there wasn't the slightest benefit to be had

from such line, once you're on the banking, you're on, and the car takes its proper line automatically.

"Incidentally, it shouldn't be supposed that Montlhèry is so designed that a car can more or less find its own way round. That would be the case only if the straights themselves were slightly banked. In point of fact, being as short as they are, the straights should be banked, and no doubt they would be, but for the way in which the Linas-Montlhèry road circuit joins the Autodrome proper. It is the extreme suddenness of the change from dead level to steep banking, and vice versa, that makes the French track a teaser. The rest is easy."

An Amazing Escape

I next introduced the subject of the crash that very nearly brought Mrs. Hawkes's career to an abrupt end a few years ago. It happened a split second after she had completed her famous Montlhèry lap record of 147.2 m.p.h. Here is the story of one of the most amazing escapes in the history of high-speed motoring, and the events leading up to it, in the words of the one best qualified to tell it.

65

1928 Amilcar at speed on the banking at Montlhèry Autodrome near Paris, which was opened in 1924. The artist is Leo Hum.

Louis Chiron, Chevalier of the Legion of Honour and Philippe Etancelin, one of the "gentleman" professionals who came to prominence in the twenties.

LOUIS CHIRON

"Our idea was to kill two birds with one stone – break the lap record and test out some Bosch plugs of a new type. As you probably know, the only way to learn anything useful from the condition of plugs is to cut the power off dead when the engine is working at its maximum revs. and temperature.

This is a three-fold process: slip into neutral, press the cut-out button, turn off the fuel tap. And all these motions must be made as near simultaneously as makes no difference. Naturally, it involves removing one hand from the wheel, and the grip of the other hand on the rim must be half relinquished in order to 'button'.

Quandary at 160 m.p.h.!

"I had done this many times before, but in the past it had always been possible to time it to coincide with one or other of the bankings. On this occasion things worked out rather differently. As the car approached the finishing line at the end of the record-breaking lap, I could see by the rev. counter that the engine

PHILIPPE ETANCELIN

was turning over faster than ever. Incidentally, it is a characteristic of these Derby motors that they go on increasing their revs. until something bursts. On that lap, for instance, we picked up five hundred revs., although the car had had a long flying start.

"Knowing the engine to have been tuned to the nth degree, I was in something of a quandary. The finishing line occurs just where the Home Straight merges into the banking; so the question to be decided, and decided quickly, was this: should I continue flat-out for about 200 metres beyond the timing strip, taking a chance that the engine would last that far on full throttle; or should I take the risk of cutting-out, finding neutral and turning off the fuel on the trickiest part of the track, right at the finishing line? For the sake of the plug data, there could of course, be no question of easing the foot a little on completing the timed lap and then 'buttoning' later, on the banking.

"Well, I chose the second alternative. No sooner was my right hand off the wheel than

the Derby went into a colossal dry skid, spun right round, ran off the concrete on to the rough ground, back on to the track again, and finally off it for good, finishing up with its nose buried deep in a minor earthwork. At the moment these things came to pass our speed was nearer 160 than 150 m.p.h., so that even with both hands on the wheel there wouldn't have been an earthly chance of correcting with the gear lever in neutral and the motor stopped; one hand alone was less than useless.

"Anyway, we killed the two birds as per schedule: record broken and plugs perfect. That the killing stopped there was just one of these miracles. An extraordinary thing about the crash was this: although I stayed in my seat and received no impact whatever, a rib and a collar-bone were broken and a shoulder muscle torn. The doctors decided that the muscle parted as the result of sheer exertion, and the rib, no longer having the support of the muscle, snapped afterwards. No one will ever know what induced the collar-bone to break.

"I probably owe my life to the heavy rain that fell a few hours before the crash. The bank we hit, being wet, cushioned the blow just enough to make all the difference. Actually the attempt had been fixed for the preceding day, but high winds made a postponement necessary. The consequence was that when we did need their services the doctor and the ambulance were comfortably tucked up in bed and garage, respectively ....

Centrifugal Superchargers '
"The experience isn't one I should care to repeat, but, on the other hand, I was glad to have saved the engine from an almost inevitable blow-up. The engine itself was quite undamaged and the broken bits were comparatively easy to replace. The centrifugal supercharger fitted to these motors is a rather tricky contrivance if anything goes wrong. I have known my husband to spend a whole week on assembling this blower. It turns at six and a half times engine speed, which is to say six and a half times six-thousand-odd.

"Comparatively little seems to be known about centrifugal superchargers among car designers in this country, but they probably have a bigger future than they are given credit for. In the aircraft world, of course, this type of blower is very highly developed."

Track and Road Racing

"Do you find track work a more fascinating business than road racing?" I asked. "I remember you driving the Maserati-engined Derby in the 1½-litre race at Dieppe a few years ago, but your appearances on the road have been rare enough to make them conspicuous."

"No, I am very fond of road racing, as a matter of fact", Mrs. Hawkes replied. "The trouble is that in order to get anywhere, one must be able to keep constantly in practice. Nor is it any use to take up road racing seriously unless one's financial resources are almost unlimited. The driver who goes in perpetual fear of piling up his or her car, and of the bill which follows, never sets the sewage farm on fire.

"For me, the fascination of track racing lies in just one thing: going over a given course faster than anyone has gone before, or driving a given type of vehicle faster than the next fastest. It is the element of the unknown which fascinates. I'd rather not drive at all than drive a car the maximum speed of which was appreciably below the limit for the course."

* * *

The parties of the second and third parts, as legal gentry say, implied by the words " we", "our", and "us" in this article are Mrs. Hawkes's husband and Fred Cann, chief mechanic to the equipe. "Every success gained", she says, "has been the result of perfect co-operation and understanding between the three of us. The world is full of drivers, both actual and potential, but believe me, it is far from full of designers, tuners and mechanics such as the two with whom I have been associated for the past seven years."

Spoken like a man.

This Year Of Racing
By Richard Seaman

During the 1934 season I drove a K.3 Magnette for the Whitney-Straight team in most of the eleven hundred and fifteen hundred Continental races. When Straight gave up racing at the end of that season, therefore, I was faced with the necessity of setting up on my own as an independent. I was anxious to continue racing on the Continent as I much preferred this to racing in England. On the choice of a car I had two alternatives. Either I could get a big car such as an Alfa or a Bugatti and be able to compete with it in the big Grand Prix races at the risk of almost certainly being outclassed by the German cars; or I could stick to the 1½-litre class with a small

"Supersonic", an oil on board – a Roy Nockolds semi-abstract work of the late 1930s.

68

Maseratis, which are very well suited to this course, and some Bugattis.

The positions of the cars for the start of this race were decided by drawing lots. This is a practice which I consider very unfair, as it is quite probable that the fastest car in the race will be placed right at the back and the driver will have to spend several laps passing the rest of the cars; and passing, in my opinion, is the most difficult and dangerous part of racing. A much fairer way is to place the cars in order of their practice lap times, so that the fastest cars are in front and the slowest at the back.

In this race I was in about the third row and experienced considerable difficulty in getting by some of the cars which had got away in front of me. By the third lap, however, I had got a comfortable lead and settled down to drive steadily and make sure of finishing. To my horror, however, about the seventh lap the oil pressure starting dying completely away after right-hand corners. This was slowing me up considerably as I had to wait till it came up again before accelerating. As there was a lot of oil on the floor boards I diagnosed that there was a leak somewhere, and the level in the oil tank had got so low that on corners the oil was surging away from the feed pipe to the engine. As it was getting worse I had to stop and fill up, with the result that Mays, Ruesch on a Maserati, and Rose-Richards all passed me, and we finished in that order.

English car, such as an E.R.A., and probably stand a fair chance of winning something. I decided on the latter course and ordered a 1½-litre E.R.A.

I took delivery of the car about the end of May and the first race I ran in was the 2,000 c.c. class of the Grand Prix des Frontiers.

This is quite a small race, but that was all to the good as the car was brand new. It is a peculiar circuit with two fast legs and one extremely narrow gravelled section. I led the race for two laps, but a piston then burnt out and I retired. I managed, however, to get the lap record for the course for which I got a nice cup.

The next excitement was the 1,500 c.c. Eifelrennen, on the Nurburg Ring, the following week.

The first three days were spent in fitting a new piston, so that I did not get the car out till the second day's practice, which was spent in running-in. I realised, of course, that there was very strong opposition in this race, as there were not only the three "Works" E.R.A's to compete with, but some very fast

R.J.B. Seaman

My next race was at Kesselberg hill climb near Munich, a fortnight later. I sent the lorry on with the racing car from the Eifelrennen, but I returned to England and flew out again the next week, arriving the Wednesday before the hill climb, which was on Sunday. The Kesselberg is a delightful spot, the actual road leading from one mountain lake up to another, and I think it is the most beautiful venue for a racing event that I know. Here again the car misbehaved, for as I was giving it a warming up run down the road just before the actual climb one of the front brakes grabbed and locked on suddenly, bending the front axle and damaging the actuating gear. We worked fiendishly for 15 minutes to remove the broken parts from inside the drum and to disconnect the front brakes completely, with the result that I could only tour up the hill with no front brakes and a negative castor-action.

I then returned home, had the car repaired and went to Donington for the Nuffield Trophy. Exactly the same thing happened again, however, with the result that I could not start.

The following week there was the Voiturette Race at Dieppe. I did three or four laps, but the supercharger drive sheared and I had to stop at the side of the road and walk disconsolately back to the pits.

The season was now more than half over and the car had broken something in every race it had run in. I decided therefore to incorporate certain modifications from standard and to have the car prepared in future by my own mechanics.

The next race after this was the Grossglockner hill climb up a newly-built road in Austria. We had been so busy on the car since Dieppe that we did not leave London until the Tuesday night before the race. I went in the lorry with Jock Finlayson, my mechanic, and driving day and night we got to the Grossglockner in the Austrian Alps on the Thursday evening, although we had to stop to change a broken spring on the lorry. This, incidentally, is the only occasion on which my Dodge lorry has given any trouble during two seasons of motor racing all over Europe.

The Grossglockner I found a pretty tough proposition, especially as there was only time for one practice run before the race, owing to our late arrival. The hill was 20 kilometres long, rose to 8,000 feet and had a very large number of corners and only a gravel surface. The altitude made carburation rather a problem, as, owing to the rarefied atmosphere at the top of the Pass, the mixture would be much too rich on a normal setting. This entailed starting with a dangerously weak mixture at the bottom to effect a compromise. You can imagine that, taking all these circumstances into consideration, I looked forward to the day of the climb with considerable trepidation. However, this time the car went very well and I won the 1,500 c.c. racing car class and was second to Tadini in a Ferrari Alfa in the general classification.

We then went on to Italy for the Coppa Acerbo at Pescara. The two mechanics, Finlayson and Evans, took the lorry, while I went in my V.8 Ford with Tony Birch, who had

now joined me as manager. Birch is the best racing manager I have ever known and our subsequent successes were very largely due to his efforts.

We went first to Milan, where we utilised the old Straight stables' garage to prepare the car for Pescara. The Pescara circuit is a very interesting one, consisting of two very fast straights of about five miles each joined by a twelve miles section of extremely twisty and undulating road which comes immediately after the pits. At the start I was in the second row, but made quite a good get away and had only Tufanelli on a Maserati ahead of me at the first corner. He was going very fast and I could not pass him until the beginning of the first straight, where his motor passed out leaving me with a good lead, which I had no difficulty in retaining until the finish.

Ten days after Pescara there was the Prix de Berne, also a race for 1,500 c.c. cars where the "factory" E.R.A's were also running. Birch and I had a wonderful trip over the Alps, the Ford's acceleration on the passes being most

TAZIO NUVOLARI

LUIGI FAGIOLI

Few makes have ever achieved the fame and popularity of Ettore Bugatti's motor cars from Molsheim. Recognised as the thoroughbreds that they were and attracting the attention of a formidable list of drivers.

Far left. The greatest driver in the history of motor racing in this writer's view. Tazio Nuvolari, the "Mantovano Volante".

Left. "The old Abruzzi Robber". Grand Prix ace Luigi Fagioli.

Protos entered for the 1908 New York race, coming second. The Berlin firm was regarded as one of the better makes on the home front in the years before the Kaiser War.

Raymond Mays, Shelsley Walsh exponent and Brooklands track star, winning the 1937 Empire Trophy Race in an ERA (English Racing Automobiles) at Donington.

impressive. The mechanics' trip in the lorry was not such a picnic, as they had to reverse the lorry on all the hairpins of the St. Gotthard Pass except two. Berne, I consider, is almost the ideal circuit. It is about five miles round, has an enormous permanent grand stand and most luxurious pits. It is mostly composed of fast bends with only two slow corners. On the first day of practice our carburation was hopeless and very difficult to rectify as all the symptoms seemed to contradict each other. The next day we got it right, but too late for any serious practice that day. The trouble was that the fuel was rather different from that which we had used in Italy. The third day was wet, so that I did not get an opportunity of practising very fast, and had to be content with a place in the second row at the start, since for this race the practice times decided your starting position. On the day of the race it was not actually raining, although the road was still wet. I got away from the start in second place behind Mays, but I was able to pass him before the end of the first lap. I increased my lead until I was about a minute ahead and I then slowed down and held this lead until the finish. "Bira" was second on another E.R.A., while Lord Howe was third with his Delage, after a simply magnificent drive on this wonderful old car.

From Berne we went on to the hill climb at Freiburg, which is known as the Grand Prix hill climb of Germany. Mays also came with his E.R.A. It is a wonderful hill, tarred all the way up and is eight miles long, but it is very twisty and takes a lot of learning. As Freiburg is only 80 miles from Berne we arrived on Monday evening and I immediately got down to learning the hill really thoroughly by riding up and down it in the Ford.

On my first practice run in the E.R.A. I went up fairly slowly to see that the car was running all right. On the second climb I went up faster and did it in 8 mins. 40 secs., which was quite satisfactory and well inside the class record. I realised, however, that the first gear band of the self-changing gearbox was rather worn, so I decided not to practise any more and to save it for the day of the climb. Sunday

was a beautiful day and there was an enormous and enthusiastic crowd. I made a very bad start with much too much wheel spin, as the tar was more slippery than I thought. I had endeavoured before this event to obtain one of the self-locking differentials as used by the Auto-Unions and Mercedes and also by Raymond Mays in hill climbs, but I had been unsuccessful in getting one. The result was that the whole way up I had terrific wheel spin, but I gave the car all she had got and she has never gone better. On arriving at the top I found I had done 8 mins. 25 1/5 secs., the fastest time so far. Mays came up with 8.36 which was second fastest. I then had a very exciting wait for the arrival of Stuck in the Auto-Union, whose best practice time had been 8.30, so that there was quite a chance that I might have beaten him. The crowd and the other drivers were all very excited and I think they would genuinely have liked to see me beat the Auto-Union. Stuck, however,

Italian Voiturette famous for providing the great Tazio Nuvolari with his first entry into motor sport.

73

Two aces who came to fame as independents in the early thirties. Algerian Marcel Lehoux and Frenchman Réné Dreyfus.

MARCEL LEHOUX

RENE DREYFUS

74

came up in 8.24 1/5, just a second better than my time. The crowd gave me a very sporting ovation on the way down the hill and altogether I noticed an entirely different attitude to that adopted towards Continental drivers who come over to this country.

The next week I was to drive one of the Evans' Magnettes in the T.T. As I did not know the circuit and the official practice time was rather short, I was anxious to arrive as soon as possible. I therefore motored into Basle that evening and caught the 9 o'clock plane on Monday morning, which landed me at Belfast at 4 o'clock that afternoon, and gave me plenty of time to get ready for the T.T. The pit organisation, under the direction of the Evans' father, was really first class. Mr. Evans had even had wireless fitted to the cars so that he could give verbal instructions to the drivers. We did not use them in the race owing to technical difficulties which arose. Although I had a trouble-free run I could do no better than tenth place.

My next race was the "500" in which I drove Jack Duller's Duesenberg with Featherstonhaugh. The car had a marvellous engine and made excellent progress while Buddy was

driving, but my thirteen stone was evidently too much for the chassis, for the rear cross-member supporting the tank collapsed as soon as I took over and our day's motoring was finished.

The following week I was to run in the 1,500 c.c. class of the Masaryk G.P. in Czecho-slovakia, so the morning after the "500" I set off in the Ford for Dover, accompanied by Tommy Clark, fully recovered from his alarming contretemps with the Bugatti wheel the day before, and Giulio Ramponi. Ramponi had been responsible for modifying the car after Dieppe, and since then the car had been prepared under his supervision, though he had never actually come abroad with me. This time, however, he was able to get away and came with me. Birch and Finlayson had already left in the lorry. We all arrived in Brno on Wednesday and found that some of the 30 kilometres circuit had been improved since last year. Most of it, however is still extremely difficult, being hilly, narrow and exceedingly bumpy. Many of the corners are made very tricky by the bumps, as the front of a light racing car is liable to be thrown right across the road on a bend. This I regret to say

happened to me on my very first warming-up lap when I was motoring round quite slowly, thinking more about the behaviour of the engine than of actual driving, with the result that I hit a kerb very hard on one of these bumpy corners. Although I had hit it quite a clout the only damage was two bent wheels and a bent hub. We had no spare hub, so Ramponi worked miracles to straighten it, though everyone said it was impossible. Fate was obviously in rather a trying mood, for the next day the brakes failed completely as I was approaching a corner and it was more by good luck than good management that I pulled up. The mechanism had failed on one brake, and as it is a fully compensated system there were no brakes left at all.

This race was 260 miles long which was the longest I had ever attempted in the E.R.A., so I was doubtful how it would stand up, especially on such a circuit, but the car went magnificently again and I did not have much difficulty in winning with plenty in hand from Veyron on a Bugatti.

This was my last race of the season, but I cannot complete this account without drawing attention to the work of Birch, Ramponi and Finlayson, who contributed so largely towards these successes in their respective capacities. I think you would have to go a long way to find a better motor-racing team than these three.

Racing in Switzerland. The artist is Armin Bieber.

V. GROSSER
PREIS DER SCHWEIZ
BERN, 21. AUG. 1938
KÜMMERLY & FREY BERN

If You Want To Be A Racing Driver
By Rudolf Caracciola 1935

Almost every post brings me letters from enthusiastic young drivers who want to become world's champions. They ask me what are the qualifications to be a racing driver and how can they learn to do high-speed driving. To tell them how to learn to do high-speed driving is difficult; that is only achieved by practice and experience; but the question as to what are the qualifications is easy to answer. The racing driver must be a born artist. As a musician is born to know by instinct what is best in music, so is the racing driver born to know what is best in driving. Out of a hundred young men who write to me perhaps three or four of them are very good drivers, but it is doubtful whether one of them is an artist. As with a violin only an artist can tell when he is getting the very best out of his instrument, and so only an artist can tell when he is getting the best out of his motor car.

The racing driver must know himself and his car. He must know the extreme limit that he can go with safety. Many chances of success on the racing track are ruined because the driver does not know enough about his machine. The maximum of every component part of the engine, must be in the mind of the driver. A little overdriving has often set a motor car on fire or burst the tyres on the next bend. When such happens the race is lost whereas knowledge of the car would have enabled the driver to carry on with the car going at its maximum, and yet never ruining his chance by trying to force the machine to do what is too much for it.

But the knowledge of the car is no use unless the driver can sense when the car is reaching its limit. Nothing can tell him, he must be able to feel by the motion of the car and by the sound of the engine when he is at his maximum. There is no time to look at the indicators on the dashboard. On an awkward bend to take your eyes off the track to look at the speedometer might prove fatal. In a tenth of a second a driver can falter enough to carry him straight off the course. The result of driving head-on into a wall or shooting clean over the edge of some banking is not hard to imagine.

The driver can never be a success unless he is prepared to use his mind as much as his body. The man who seizes the wheel, sets his teeth and blinds off up the track can never be successful when he is competing against a driver who is thinking hard before the race starts and continues to do so until it is over. In a moment he has to sum up the position and think out which is the best course to take. How without ruining his car by a burst of speed at the beginning, he can get to the front of the other competitors, and what is more, how he can keep there. It is not all a matter of the power of his car; in nine cases out of ten it is the man at the wheel who wins or loses a race.

Knowledge of the track is an indispensable factor in successful motor racing. This can only be obtained by practising on the track itself before a race takes place. If a driver does not know the track it is impossible for him to know how to use his car to get the best out of it. I have made it my business to get to know every race track in Europe, but even so, I would not set out on any of them for a race without having had a trial spin first. Too many drivers make the mistake of only getting to know the track under one condition of weather. It is not at all unusual for a race to start in brilliant sunshine and to finish in torrential rain. The driver who has only tried the track in fine weather is beaten the moment the rain comes; and in many races the drivers retire rather than drive on over a slippery surface that they do not know.

Too much practice can never come the way of the racing driver. He should be at the wheel day in and day out. As it is impossible for him always to be driving an enormous Mercedes-Benz or some other well-known racing car, the best practice he can possibly get is to do a lot of private motoring. Experience on the highroad will serve a man well when he comes to the track. Particularly beneficial is it to drive in heavy traffic, for the start of a race,

77

on which so very much always depends, is very similar to starting up when the traffic indicator says "Go" at Hyde Park Corner. The only difference is that on the track it is all done much quicker, but the method adopted is just the same. Private driving is also one of the best forms of practice, if not the only form, for long-distance endurance races.

Unless a youth, for the racing driver must start young, has excellent physique it is no use him thinking of taking up motor racing. Racing is a terrific strain on the body and on the nerve system which only a strong man can stand. If you are in the least bit nervous, drop the idea. of racing at once.

The work of the driver is very hard. It involves much more than just sitting at a wheel for a few hours a week while thousands of people stand round and cheer. My own experience has shown me that it is a full time job involving a good many more hours of labour than most of the more common means of earning a livelihood. From March to November I spend every Sunday driving in a trial or race, and during the rest of the week I am out on practice runs or spending several hour a day driving my private car for traffic and endurance practice. During the months between November and March I keep fit by playing winter sports, as I find these are at one and the same time a relaxation after the past season's racing and yet a training for the coming season.

Never become a racing motorist unless you are a natural sport. This I know applies to all sports, but in my case I love cars as well as the sport of racing, and even when I do not win a race I enjoy the race for the sheer pleasure of working in conjunction with a wonderful car. Young drivers, before you take to racing as a livelihood, or as a sport, remember that you are risking your lives every time you go on the track. But if you are fit, keen and prepared to work hard, you will find nothing to compare with motor racing. It's a wonderful life.

WITH HANS STUCK AT SHELSEY WALSH
1936

It was between the first and second climbs. The shrill, exhilarating exhaust notes of competing cars were now but memories, and over all brooded an exaggerated silence.

The paddock was deserted, save for the inevitable bustle of mechanics and drivers endeavouring to get their cars ready for the next run.

Heavy rain during the latter stages of the first climb explained the discrepancies in the times set up by some of the smaller cars and of the big stuff; and the man whom everyone expected again to lower the record of the hill had been unable to do so on a road churned as slippery as ice-rink.

When I found his car, its terribly disappointed crowd of mechanics had just finished "going over" it. "What a pity he couldn't show them", they were muttering. " – bad propaganda for Germany and the Auto-Union."

I explained that the people of this country were thrilled by the beauty of the car and fully

**Rudolf Caracciola.
Artistic perfection in
Grand Prix driving.**

RUDOLF CARACCIOLA

der erfolgreichste Rennfahrer der Welt

deutscher Meister und Europameister 1935 und 1937

auf

MERCEDES · BENZ

Bugatti. One of the most attractive "classic" outlines ever adopted for a motor car.

Hillclimbing in Switzerland.

understood how impossible it was for him to do anything on the wet and narrow road. I had a look at the car. The whole job seemed just to have come out of a showroom – not a speck of oil on engine or chassis.

The rev-counter dial, I noticed, goes up to 5,500 only. From 3,500 to 4,250 the figures are green; from 4,250 to 5,000 yellow, and the rest red.

I asked them about the driver. They did not know where he was. I thought it strange that his presence was not indicated somewhere by a crowd of interested people, and thus pondering, went in search of him.

It was in the hay barn, where the private cars were parked, that I finally found him, sitting in his beautiful black 5-litre Horch – alone.

He looked dejected, yet it was the same Hans Stuck I had met over and over again on the Continent.

The first time I met him was when we were fellow competitors, in 1928 in a race at the Nurburg Ring. Racing seems strangely

rejuvenating. He had changed little, but cars have become faster since.

In 1928 his Austro-Daimler clocked 120 m.p.h. Now his new mount holds five world's records and does a genuine 200 m.p.h. on the road.

In 1928 he had just been coming into the limelight. His old rival and friend, Caracciola with the S.S. Mercedes, went from victory to victory until Stuck put a stop to it in hill climbs with an unsupercharged car of half the cylinder capacity!

He had made fastest time of the day in the Nurburg race in heavy rain on a road which was as narrow as the Shelsley course, and lined with parkland – and the surface was clay, strewn with a thin layer of gravel. Every driver had looked the same after that race, I remembered, his face crusted with mud and his mouth filled with sand.

We talked about mutual friends, and I remembered how difficult it had been for him really to get going at the start of his career. Austro-Daimler lent him one of their unblown 19-100 6-cylinder three-litre cars for races. And the car had promptly packed up in two of them! Then came the first Eifel race in 1927 when he finished third in his class. This had made it easier for him to convince the Austro-Daimler directors of his qualities.

After that he had got a shorter chassis and success began to come his way.

Twice he was English Hill Climbing Champion, in 1930 and again in 1931. The following year he joined Mercedes-Benz, and when the building of Grand Prix cars brought the dawn of a new era to German racing he joined the Auto-Union concern.

His English is excellent and he prefers to use it whenever he is over here.

"What do you think of the Hill?" I asked him.

"Oh, all right", was his guarded rejoinder.

"Do you find it different from 1930?"

"No, not at all, only the surface is much better."

"Do you think the S-bend is really difficult to tackle?"

"Well, it is not easy, but the most difficult

and dangerous point on the course undoubtedly is the bump with the slight left-hand bend just before the S. It is a pity I could not make use of the horse-power at my disposal, but really my wheels never gripped the hill the whole way up. I had to keep her going that's all. Mays was fortunate in getting his run in dry weather."

"Do you think you would have beaten the record?"

"I am confident I would. You see yesterday in a practice run I was clocked at one second faster than the record and I am sure I could have knocked off a couple of seconds on a dry day."

He gazed up at the sky with its clouds devoid of silver lining, and I hastened to tell him that sometimes we have quite a nice summer here with genuine sunshine. He looked at me with doubt in his eyes.

"Is it very difficult to drive one of the Auto-Unions?" I asked him. "No, not really," he answered, "only you want an entirely new technique. You must understand that the car

Manufacture d'amiante H. DOUHA-DOR. Liège.

is behind and not in front of you – like driving a London bus", he added. "Whenever you approach a bend you have to go into it much later. If you go into a bend too soon then you find the tail coming round at you and you can't help getting into a spin. That's what happened to Rosemeyer. He has plenty of courage, mind you but he has still to get used to the new technique. Yesterday in Barcelona he did it again and went up a lamp-post!"

"That reminds me. Do you think that the modern Grand Prix car is more dangerous than its prototype – cars such as the 2.3 Bugattis, for instance?"

"Of course there is really no comparison possible between the modern Auto-Union and the oldtime Bug. But I think definitely that racing is no more dangerous now than it used to be. The only difference is that you have to think quicker."

"What do you think of English drivers?" I next asked him.

"They are extremely good on small cars – and those small cars of theirs are amazing", was his reply.

I told him that the new Austins were reputed to rev. up to 12,000 r.p.m. He seemed surprised and commented: "I think they must get their best power output at about 7,000 revs., the balance of revs. being in the nature of a safety margin to safeguard the gear boxes".

My question as to whether or not his car differed from other Auto-Unions elicited the fact that, apart from its smaller petrol tank and its 200m. shorter wheel base, it is identical with the rest.

I told him that we had been afraid that he would have to start in Barcelona.

"My directors did not want to let me come to England", he replied, "but I told them I had promised to come, and so here I am!"

"What do you think of Donington?"

"It's too narrow. We would all like to come over and race here provided we could have a suitable course and better prize-money and so on. You can tell your race promoters this: they could have any number of the best Grand Prix drivers and their cars as soon as they really

Advertising for brakes in Dutch from Cappiello. This version was also known as the "old nail" poster.

81

cater for them. It is a thousand pities England has no Grand Prix race.

"The sporting enthusiasm of the drivers and spectators is marvellous, but they do not seem to have a proper outlet for it. It seems also that motor racing in England is governed by red tape. For instance, I wanted to have a shot at the Brooklands Lap Record, but the track authorities insisted on my fitting a special silencer to my car. This would mean an enormous amount of work and practically no reward if I were successful".

"Do you really think that you could have taken the Brooklands Record?"

"Sure," he replied confidently. "I think I could raise the figure to something between 180 and 190 m.p.h."

"But that's impossible. The banking isn't steep enough for such speed."

"Possibly not in most cars," said Stuck, "but my car holds the road in an amazing manner and she does 200 m.p.h. and therefore I feel certain I could easily have taken the Brooklands Lap Record. Already I hold 50 km. and 50 mile records, and 100 km. and 100 miles. I got those on one of the new concrete motor roads, and in getting the two latter records it was necessary for me to turn round on the second half of the run because the road between Heidelberg and Darmstadt is only 50 miles long."

"Talking of records, will you come back again in September?"

"No, I am afraid I cannot. Unfortunately the date of the September climb clashes with that of the Italian Grand Prix and as I won that event last year, I must defend my title."

"Will you come back again?"

"I cannot tell definitely. I should like to, but it all depends on the International Calendar."

Jenatzy wins the 1903 Gordon Bennett race (actually the tyres were from Continental).

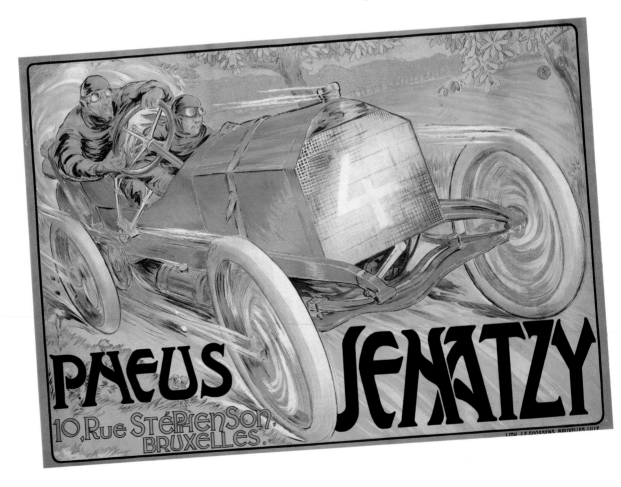

Master mould for a
Blitzen Benz by
Vittorio Guttner.
Germany 1912.

To Give Audible Warning
1907

The great difficulty that one has to make vehicular traffic aware of a car's approach is well known to all motorists. Covered vans and other slow-moving vehicles are the chief obstacles in this respect, and the ordinary horn is at times of very little use when one desires to overtake such traffic. Horse drivers generally keep in the middle of the road, and fail to hear the blowing of the horn. This often means the overtaking car slowing right down, and the occupants shouting for all they are worth. The driver of the cart, when this stage is reached, realises that there is some thing behind him, and slowly draws to the proper side of the road, allowing the car to go ahead.

A solution of the problem is the utilisation of an electric horn, of which a number of different types are now being placed on the market. One of the best known is perhaps the Wagner. We recently fitted an electric horn of this make to one of our cars, with exceedingly satisfactory results. The difficulty of overtaking traffic mentioned above is at once overcome; drivers of horse vehicles and other forms of traffic, upon the sound of the horn, at once betake themselves to their own side. We do not intend to describe the working of the Wagner horn, as it was only in our issue of September 15th, 1906 that we did so. Suffice to say that the necessary electric current is supplied by an eight-volt or two four-volt accumulators. The switch is conveniently placed on the steering wheel, and additional ones can be fitted in the tonneau, so that the passengers occupying the rear seats can work the instrument. The advantages of having the means of working the horn so handy cannot be overestimated. The button can be pressed without taking the hand off the steering wheel, even though one may be in the act of changing speed at the same time with the other.

Another advantage that the Wagner, in common with other electric horns, possesses is that it can be kept on for any length of time. In traffic, the electric horn scores on this point over its predecessor, which one cannot keep blowing continuously; you blow the horn, and then you have to wait for a second or so whilst the bulb fills with air again. The note produced by the Wagner electric horn may be tuned to suit one's taste.

The Wagner electric horn under review was obtained from the United Motor Industries.

83

E. R. HALL

M.G. and Bentley were campaigned by the ever popular Eddie Hall.

THE RECORD
By John Little
1936

Hans Klausen sat on the tailboard of the works lorry and surveyed the scene around him with misgiving.

All the paraphernalia of the famous Haslingford hill-climb lay wide open to his view. On either side, racing cars of all sizes, makes and colours were parked on the grass of the paddock, many of them with their bonnets open as the owners carried out frenzied last-minute adjustments, while others emitted fumes and snarls as they were warmed up for their run.

Spare wheels, tools, cans of petrol, discarded wings and all the other mysterious impedimenta inseparable from a motor sport event, were spread out on the green, while white-overalled figures moved amongst the cars, and the air was full of the familiar smell of racing oil and doped fuel.

Away on his right, the course itself, a narrow road of rather bumpy asphalt, wound its way between low grassy banks, lined now with spectators, up into a fold of the Downs.

As he looked, a single-seater M.G. Midget was on the starting line yelping like an excited puppy as its driver waited for the flag. Hans watched it while the flag fell, the yelp became a snarl, and the little blue car scuttled off up the hill.

He brought his gaze back to his immediate surroundings and shuddered. Just below him, ringed by interested spectators, who at this free-and-easy meeting could wander where they pleased, lay the sleek white single-seater Zeidler which he was to drive in the unlimited class.

News of the entry of this car had made the attendance larger than usual, for it was one of a make famed throughout the racing world, which had carried all before it on the Continent. The chance of seeing one in England, and, furthermore, at close quarters, had brought enthusiasts from miles around. Now, as they watched the two mechanics changing the plugs and getting the car ready, there was

much speculation amongst them as to why this big German firm had gone to the expense of sending over car, mechanics and driver to a relatively small meeting like this.

Hans Klausen heard them, and shuddered again; he knew only too well why it was.

He was being given a last chance to rehabilitate himself after a dreadful moment in the Drochenberg Grand Prix, when he had nearly lost the race for his team by becoming suddenly frightened of the blasting noise and the speed. The speed ... the speed .... It was still vivid in his mind.

He had just managed to stop at the Zeidler pit, had been hauled out of the cockpit, shaking and incoherent, while Fritz Keller, his co-driver, had climbed cursing in again and gone off for another three-hour spell to win the race.

One lap! Oh God, only one lap had finished him, and he had nearly crashed on that. His had been the only one of the three team cars left in the race – the others had engine troubles – but Keller had put it in a leading

position, and he had only to drive steadily to win … but somehow the speed had got him down. Strange, because he had won several races in slower cars, and the Zeidler people had thought enough of him to try him in their first-line team.

And now here he was, with the words of old Birnbaum, the team manager, still ringing in his ears:

"Now look, Klausen. We're sending you over to England, to the Haslingford hill-climb, with one of the team cars. It will be easily the fastest car there, and we expect you to lower the record. I still believe you can handle the car all right, and in any case, this isn't like a Grand Prix; you'll have the road to yourself, and you can get your confidence back.

"Now go and do it. Come home with the record, and I'll persuade the directors to try you in the team again. It wants some getting, but come back without it, and as far as we're concerned you're finished."

Hans sighed. He was lucky to be given this chance. Not many firms would have done it

but Zeidlers were making big profits, and took their sporting side very seriously, as a good advertisement, so they were spending this money on the chance of finding another good driver, and getting the record as well.

His thoughts came back to the present with a snap. One of the mechanics was calling him, and from a nearby loud-speaker he caught the announcer's words: "… ready now for Class 12 racing cars unlimited … will cars 7, 9, 14, 17, 18, 32, 38, 44 and 51 come to the start, please".

He was No. 51. The entry had been late, and he would be the last runner in his class. He slid off the tailboard and walked up to his car, which the mechanics had turned round and pushed to the top of the little road leading to the starting line. Walking beside it, as they rolled it down the slight slope, he looked at it and felt a cold chill once more. So much power, such terrific acceleration, and … such a narrow road. Not like a Grand Prix, no, but had not a famous driver said that these short runs were as exacting as a long race, because

the smallest mistake was fatal to success ? Hell, he must do it, he must ....

But now things were happening. The announcer's voice came again to his ears: "... Car No. 32 is on the line.... Mr. W. H. Ashton's 'Special', the Thunderbolt .... as most of you will know, this car holds the record for the course, and as it has been rebuilt since its last appearance here .... Ah, he's off ... beautiful start". Hans watched with interest as Ashton hurtled away, the peculiar booming exhaust note characteristic of all his cars echoing from the surrounding hills.

He disappeared round the corner half-way up the course, and came into view again, a flying red shape, near the finish. "Hallo everybody", roared the brazen voice. "Here is some good news. The record has been broken. Mr. Ashton made the very fine time of 38 2/5 seconds that is, 1 3/5 seconds under his own old record This looks like being an exciting afternoon, as Herr Klausen is here with a V-8 Zeidler, entered by the works, and we may expect a very fast run from him."

All the spectators within range turned and looked again at Hans and his car, seeing only a grave, brown-faced young German, whose expression gave no hint of his inner feelings.

The record broken already! He would have to go all out to better Ashton's new time. He wished he could have practised on the course, but that was not allowed here.

He had walked up it, naturally, but that wasn't the same .... There was a nasty bump on one of the corners, and he couldn't remember which ... it would be awkward if he hit that fast, and unprepared. He became aware of a movement in the crowd. The R.A.C. steward, a genial, tubby man, was walking up the course, almost begging people to stand further back from the ropes. Presently the announcer started on the same task: "Ladies and gentlemen will you please get back from the edge of the bank there .... I can see some small boys right under the ropes ... we've got some very fast cars coming up now, and if you won't stand back we shall have to abandon the meeting". Everybody chuckled, the usual

threat. They moved back good-humouredly and waited.

Where was this famous Zeidler ? That was what they wanted – the real thoroughbred.

A marshal came up to Hans.

"Ready, Herr Klausen?"

Hans nodded and levered himself into his narrow cockpit and switched on his petrol pumps and ignition. The car preceding him had just got off the line. He slipped into gear and held out his clutch while the mechanics pushed ... speed enough ... the clutch went in, and the engine came alive with a blaring howl from the wide fish-tails astern.

The massed spectators heard it, and fell over one another to get closer to the ropes; this was a real car. Bill Ashton heard it and frowned – it sounded too good, would his record fall so soon? ... the attendant mechanics heard it and grinned happily, their car was in perfect tune ....

They pushed her up to the line, where a boy thrust chocks under a back wheel. Hans slipped his goggles over his eyes and prayed. Now ... the starter was raising his little Union Jack ... first gear in, clutch just free, engine revving nicely .... Right. The starter's arm fell with a jerk.

Down went Hans' right foot, up his left ... the tip of the rev-counter needle dived rapidly to the bottom of its circle checked momentarily as the clutch went home, and began to climb up the other side, while the car fled off the mark like a catapult-launched aeroplane.

"Gosh", murmured a young enthusiast on the ropes, "what a start ... if only I could do that ...."

Hans, now in second gear, felt happier. He'd got away perfectly, and his screaming acceleration was making him less uncomfortable than he had expected. The first corner loomed up and he held the car into it easily.

"It's going to be all right", ran his thoughts, "It's going to be ... hell." With a paralysing chill of horror he remembered where the bump was; right on the second corner, and he was placed all wrong for it ....

His mind panicked momentarily, but sub-

the motor, fitted a new piston and new cylinder, having the car ready for the race, all in thirty minutes. Burman was then allowed to make three trial laps while the race was held up, and then the event was started. Resta was the ultimate winner, with Oldfield second and "Wild Bob" a close third. He would undoubtedly have won if a tyre change, costing him 16 seconds, had not been necessary.

Two races were scheduled for the Sheepshead Bay Speedway in New York on November 2nd, 1915. One of them was a four-mile match race between Ralph De Palma in a 12-cylinder Sunbeam and Rob Burman in his world's record holding Blitzen Benz. De Palma won by two-tenths of a second ahead of Burman, the average speed being 111.9 m.p.h. Then came a 100-mile event which was won by Dario Resta, with Burman seven seconds back of him.

The chequered flag

On April 8th, 1916, while only five laps from the finish of a race at Corona, California, the career of Bob Burman came to an abrupt end. He was in second place gaining fast when a tyre blew out while his Peugeot was travelling upwards of 105 m.p.h. The car turned over, killing both driver and mechanic. Thus passed a great American driver whose victories were a belated reward for persistence.

He had reached the crest he sought for many years, and passed on as he wished: behind the wheel of a racing car. The spirit of speed has been transmitted through his family to his daughter, who to-day, living in California, participates with distinction in the field of motor boat racing.

ROAD WARNINGS
1907

Your thanks and the thanks of automobilists generally are due to those of our readers who send us intimations of police traps, or bad or dangerous sections of roads. We are, of course, always pleased to insert particulars of those warnings and it would also be a con-

venience if readers would inform us of the discontinuance of any traps when such withdrawals come to their knowledge. We are informed on reliable authority that the police are about to work traps between Hungerford and Marlborough, on the Bath Road, with an electric timing device apparatus, also a night trap, which detecting any driver driving more than eight miles per hour, will cause proceedings to be taken. Numbers of all cars passing through Marlborough are already being regularly taken.

MOTOR RACING GRAMOPHONE RECORDS
1935

For information regarding gramophone recordings of motor racing, the Gramophone Co. of Hayes publish a series of stage effect records on H.M.V. discs, one of which has ordinary motor car noises included, but I am not certain if there are any with the particular sounds which Mr. Exley requires. The price of these records is 5s. per disc double-sided. The Columbia Co. also make records of this nature. I would add that if your correspondent wishes to play these in public he will require a licence issued by the manufacturer and one from the Performing Rights Society. Hoping that this will be of use.

The Belle Epoque. Peugeot were one of the earliest names to commission poster art.

95

GOOD DRIVING OR GOOD RACING DRIVING IS NOT A MATTER OF SEX
1933

Many male motorists I know start a "moan" about the woman driver whenever anybody driving a car does anything silly or thoughtless on the roads. They immediately give their war cry of "I bet that's a woman"; quite often when they arrive opposite the offending car they discover the driver to be a man, but this fact does not soften their judgment of the woman driver.

I often wonder how many men who teach their wives or sisters to drive – I do not include other men's wives and sisters, because a man, strange to relate, usually has so much more patience with friends than with members of his own family – do the job properly, and how many just teach the woman to steer and scramble through the gears, so that it is a relief for her to get into top gear; so much so that she usually stays there too long, with a horror of changing down.

Another thing which the male motorists sometimes overlook is the fact that a few years ago women more or less all began to drive together, so that there was an enormous number of women on the road making the usual beginner's mistakes. On that quite a lot of male drivers based their opinion of the woman motorist – despite the fact that to-day on the roads one usually finds the woman a perfectly normal driver.

Good motor driving or motor racing not being a question of sex at all, but just mentality, I always long for a large hammer when I hear a man slanging women motorists en masse.

Running Boards in Favour Again

Women motorists will be glad of the return to favour of the running board. Recently I have covered a good many miles in two different motor cars equipped with running boards instead of just steps. I could not help noticing how clean these two cars have remained whilst being driven about in all kinds of weather.

One of them was a cream and black Armstrong Siddeley sports saloon which has amazingly good "mudguarding", and keeps its spick and span appearance even after a week of motoring in our changeable climate.

Mrs. Victor Bruce, aviatrix, speedboat pilot and accomplished driver who secured numerous records between the two world wars.

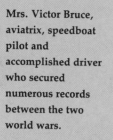

A sporting light
Salmson portrayed by
Réné Vincent.

Very litte dirt and mud gets on to the body. And, most essential of all, the screen keeps clean, an item which has not been found in some recent designs. Numerous cars which I have driven during bad weather get their windscreens into an appalling mess with mud thrown up by the car through inefficient mudguarding. Even the best of windscreen wipers cannot clear mud off a screen.

The other car, which, by the way, has reverted to running boards, is the new M.G. Magna. Last year this car was without. The appearance of the car is actually improved by the extra mud protection provided by the running boards, for the sweep of the wings, one line from front to rear, is a delight to the eye. And, of course, such a car will keep much cleaner, a thing which a woman owner-driver who does her own weekly wash down will appreciate.

Gears Still Not Used Efficiently

Nearly every week I drive up Reigate Hill, and a thing that surprises me is the fact that very few drivers seem to get the best out of their cars climbing this once famous "test hill". The majority of drivers wait until the engine is dying before changing down, and the result is that they lose revs and in the end have to drop down to an even lower gear than should have been necessary.

They do not seem to realise that to change early with the engine revving comfortably will mean that they can climb the hill on a higher gear than if they lose all power by letting the engine labour. Apart from which, of course, is the fact that it is much pleasanter if the engine is turning over nicely. As the easy-change gear boxes become yet more popular drivers will get the full benefit from their gears.

An advertisement for Bleriot lamps.

RACING IMPROVES THE BREED

Raising dust, records

and the spectators' pulsebeats

The biggest name in Automobile art is Frederick Gordon Crosby.

Lautenschlager's winning Mercedes passes Szisz, losing rim and tyre on the Renault during the 1908 French Grand Prix. A field of 46 starters saw 23 retirements.

Each country was represented by three cars involving no more than three makes for the Gordon Bennett Trophy. Théry (Brasier) is shown with Bianchi (Wolseley "Beetle") and in the background one of the "gods" Nazzaro (Fiat).

Curiosities Of Motor Racing
By R. King-Farlow

The Great British Public, aided and abetted by the lay Press, seems rather too prone to regard a racing driver as being a sort of superman, complete with nerves of steel. In actual fact anything less steely-nerved than the normal driver before the start of a big race is hard to imagine, but some drivers certainly are "tough". Witness Monsieur Cheret, a French cyclecar expert, given to competing in the Bol d'Or. There are two Bols d'Or, one for motor-cycles and the other for cars, cyclecars and three-wheelers, each of twenty-four hours' duration, one driver alone being allowed. Before 1935 these two events used to be held over the Whitsun week-end, one after the other. The motor-cycle event started on the Saturday at 4 p.m., finishing at 4 on the Sunday afternoon. Then, one hour later, the cars were sent off. In 1931 Cheret rode successfully in the motor-cycle race, winning his class, had an hour's breather and then set off for another round-the-clock jaunt on a 350 c.c. Sphinx-Staub tri-car. And he kept going and finished, again winning his class, although admittedly he was the only starter! Not content with this herculean performance, he set out the following year to repeat it. All went well with the motor-cycle, a class win being duly recorded. With the Sphinx-Staub he again got going well, but apparently dropped happily off to sleep. The tri-car shot off the road and overturned, Cheret being knocked unconscious. He came to in the ambulance tent, brooded for a while and then demanded to know if his car was smashed. On being told that it was apparently unharmed, he promptly got up, scattered the horrified nursing staff, dressed, marched back to the wreck, pushed it back to the road, got in and drove off, to complete the 24-hours without further mishap.

Pitwork records
The 1934 Twenty-four Hour Targa Abruzzo was the scene of one of the finest pieces of pitwork ever recorded. Early in the race the lead, both on distance and on formula, was taken by the 2.6-litre Ferrari Alfa, driven in turn by Guy Moll and Pietro Ghersi. Shortly after midnight, half-time, came catastrophe. Moll cruised in to his pit with a broken crown-wheel. A hurried consultation and three of the Scuderia's mechanics – Lucchi, Storchi and Del Frate – got to work under the supervision of Marinoni. Sixteen minutes and twenty seconds later, Ghersi shot off again with an entirely new back axle assembly in place! But this miraculous work, which cost the car barely a lap, availed nothing, for the new differential packed up before a single lap had been covered, this time well away from the pits.

Many records are claimed for pit-stops, but the times registered by John Cobb's team on his 24-hour record attempts at Montlhèry in 1933 and 1934 take some beating. There were several disadvantages about the Napier-Railton from the pit-work point of view. To begin with, the size and weight of the wheels slowed things down considerably. Again, owing to the size of the car, each wheel had to be jacked separately. Also the hose-pipe for refuelling was of such colossal proportions that it required at least two men to handle it. Nevertheless, the scheduled stops, comprising changing all four wheels, putting in 30 gallons of fuel and a gallon of oil, changing drivers, topping up with water, cleaning the screen, pushing the car back some distance and then pushing forward again in order to restart before the original stopping line, took well under a minute on every occasion, the best of the lot being 51 seconds dead. Of course, in record work, as opposed to races, an unlimited number of assistants may be used. Nevertheless, it is only by careful forethought, planning and drilling that a dozen or more men can work on a car simultaneously without once getting in each other's way.

Rises and falls
At the present time Alfa-Romeos are rather eclipsed by their German rivals. But a bare two years ago the Italian firm was enjoying

the biggest run of success ever known by a racing marque. From the beginning of August, 1933, till the middle of July, 1934, there was only one International event for Grand Prix cars which Alfa-Romeos failed to win, while they also annexed most of the sports car events available. The Targa Abruzzo started the ball rolling, followed by the Coppa Acerbo. Then came the Grands Prix of Comminges, Marseilles, Italy, Czechoslovakia, Spain and Monaco, the Mille Miglia, the Alessandria, Tripoli, and Casablanca Grands Prix, the Targa Florio, the Avusrennen, the Mannin Moar, the Grand Prix of Montreux, Le Mans, the Coppa Barcelona, the Grand Prix de l'A.C.F. and the Marne Grand Prix. The only failure was in the Eifelrennen, where Alfas ran third to Mercedes and Auto-Union. The final breaking of the spell came in the German Grand Prix, also held on the Eifel circuit, where the red cars of the Scuderia Ferrari again finished behind the two white German cars.

During that wonderful year Alfa-Romeos were absolutely unbeatable. Undoubtedly they had fine drivers, but the true superiority lay in the cars, for the wins were by no means the perquisite of a single pilot. Of the events listed above, Chiron won six, Varzi five, Fagioli three, Moll two, and Trossi and Lewis one each, while Chinetti and Etancelin shared the wheel at Le Mans and Severi and Cortese drove together in the Targa Abruzzo.

There have been several periods in racing history when one marque has stood out above all others of the time. In the earliest days Panhards had everything their own way. Then, for a while, F.I.A.T. swept the board. The Lion-Peugeots were unbeatable in their class for some years. The Talbots were con-

The theme of "Women and Cars" was a favourite one. The artist is Celos.

Belgian Georges Gaudy was an ex-racing cyclist and outstanding magazine illustrator.

sidered invincible in post-war years, to be followed by Delage and Bugatti. To-day Mercedes and Auto-Union collect most of the honours. None of these teams, however, established quite such a reputation as was enjoyed by the Ferrari machines at their prime. If an entry came in from the Modena stable, the result was a foregone conclusion, no matter what the opposition. If, as is hoped, the new 12-cylinder Alfa comes up to the expectations of its creators, the next competi- tion season is going to be something to be remembered for all time. Ferrari have tasted the joys of absolute supremacy, have found them very good indeed, and want more. The Germans, on the other hand, have recently approached near enough to the summit to appreciate in full its desirability, and will spare nothing to reach it. 1934 was good, 1935 better. It looks as though 1936, from the point of view of the motor racing enthusiast, will be the best of all.

Vogue magazine cover by the celebrated Georges Lepape.

America's Fastest Circuit
By Frank G. Hetishee

No doubt many of you readers find American racing confusing. For example, you read of the famed Indianapolis Sweepstakes run under the sanction of the A.A.A., and perhaps you later read of the C.S.R.A., the I.M.C.A., the A.M.R.A., the N.A.R.A., and various other racing associations. Consequently, you end up wondering what it is all about.

The A.A.A., or American Automobile Association, is generally conceded as a model for the other associations to follow; that is regarding rules on safety, track conditions, etc. The A.A.A. is the oldest association governing automobile races in the United States, and they sanction the Indianapolis Sweepstakes, the Vanderbilt Cup Race, and numerous dirt track events.

Racing Conditions

In the era of the board speedways the A.A.A. was probably at its height, but with the passing of the wooden saucers, auto racing in America dwindled down to the Indianapolis classic and the dirt tracks. It is the writer's intention to briefly summarize several of these racing associations with the hope that readers will have a better understanding of the racing conditions in America. Although the Central States Racing Association is not one of the oldest governing bodies, nevertheless, the C.S.R.A. met with popular approval with its inception back in 1935.

The originators were headed by J. K. Bailey, M.D., who at the time was president of the Dayton, Ohio, speedway. Another backer was Frank Funk, who had been promoting dirt track races since 1916 and who owned several banked oiled tracks. Others included Henry Miller, Foster Shultz, Wallace Booker, and Norman Witte.

This small group of men believed they could organize a group of tracks that would operate every week, which would enable drivers a financially profitable circuit. Knowing there would be a guaranteed purse wait-

Abnormally stout spectator by Gustav Adolf Mossa. Keeping out cold, and the dust, was a priority.

ing them each week, the drivers naturally would follow the circuit. Besides guaranteed purses, the officials saw to it that a drivers' contingency fund would take care of any unfortunate pilots that might be involved in a crash.

The I.M.C.A., or International Motor Contest Association, sanctions the majority of their races at State Fairs, Expositions, and County Fairs held throughout America. In the beginning, C.S.R.A. races consisted of Sunday meets held independently of fairs. In fact, the tracks were modelled differently from the average fair-ground track. Instead of being more or less flat on the turns, they are highly-banked bowls or saucers.

Faster Tracks

These bowls are oiled, which result in a hard top surface, free of dust. The original bowls were half-mile affairs, and grandstands overlooked then allowing spectators a full view of the speedway. With this type of track considerably more speed could be attained.

In 1936 C.S.R.A. guaranteed a minimum purse of $750 per meet. In 1937 the purse was raised to $1,000, although in the majority of cases it was considerably more than this figure. In 1938 it was raised to a minimum of $1,400, and at this writing it is already assured that the majority of C.S.R.A. meets will carry a heavier purse than the minimum.

The Dayton, Ohio, and Greenville, Ohio, speedways are both half-milers, as well as the Winchester, Indiana, and Jungle Park, Indiana, bowls. At Fort Wayne, Indiana, the track is five-eighths of a mile, and the new Hammond Raceway located just out of Chicago is also five-eighths of a mile.

The majority of race fans recall the spectacular Altoona, Pa., wooden speedway that was the scene of many hectic battles back in the gay twenties. However, with the elements of the weather and the tremendous speed of cars the Altoona boards gave up the ghost like the other wooden tracks.

Revival

In 1935 the Altoona speedway was revived when a mile-and-an-eighth track was made inside the old wooden structure. One National Championship A.A.A. race was

m.c.F = joie de la route

Period piece from Geo.Ham

held, and racing was at a standstill until Labor Day, 1937, when monied interests took over the famous old speedway under a C.S.R.A. franchise.

At this writing, two yearly races will be held at Altoona, a Flag Day classic in June, and a Labor Day grind in September.

In the past the C.S.R.A. conducted races at fairs on weekdays in the midwest which allowed drivers still time to compete on their regular Sunday dates.

Present indications point to a number of new fair dates on the 1938 schedule and reports from C.S.R.A. executive offices in Dayton appear that several promoters in the mid-west are endeavouring to secure sanctions.

Plans for 1938 call for two races on the same day in some instances, and it is expected that C.S.R.A. will invade two new States-west of the Mississippi river during the fair season.

And now something about the drivers. Everett Saylor, 1937 champion, represents one of the finest drivers in the business to-day. A college man and a former Indiana school teacher, Saylor hit his stride in 1937 and was practically unbeatable.

The former Hoosier schoolmaster started in at the bottom, and his first few years were slim, but he used his head and learned by experience.

Joie Chitwood is the only active full-blooded Indian in racing to-day. The Cherokee redskin is a fearless, nervy pilot. After the late Red Campbell met an instantaneous death in May, 1937, the plucky Indian was given the assignment of driving the former champion's Morgan Miller Special, and though getting started six weeks late in the title race, Chitwood managed to finish in second place in the 1937 title standing.

Then comes Les Adair, who often appears too fearless, and though the Indianapolis speedster has never had a really superior car to drive, he is always in the midst of things and is well up in the money when the purse is distributed.

Handsome Johnny McDowell is another nervy pilot who hails from the California

coast; Morris Musick comes from Dallas, Texas, and is always a figure to reckon with, especially in long grinds; Clay Corbitt, John DeCamp, Henry Schlooser, Buzz Mendenhall, Duke Dinsmore, Gordon Chard, Paul Russo, Bayless Leverett, Larry Beckett, Mike Salay, John Tersinor, Everett Rice are but a few of the many fine men competing on the banks.

Procedure

The usual procedure of a meet starts with the time trials, which find each driver warming up and then being timed for one lap. After all cars are qualified, they are lined up for a beauty selection. The crowds in the stands applaud their favourite car and crew, and the one receiving the greatest ovation receives a cash prize, while the second and third receive a smaller amount.

Next comes a series of four or more spring races of ten laps, and the first three finishers in each event are automatically placed in line for the feature race of the afternoon. Sometimes a ten-lap handicap race is run with the slower qualifiers placed ahead of the fastest. Usually by 4 p.m. the feature event is

Rossotti's interpretation of "Women and Cars".

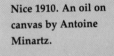

about ready to be run. In this, cars are lined up two abreast. After all cars are started, the drivers make a few laps warming up their cars and getting into their proper positions.

When they are all in their places, the starter gives them the flag and away they go. Feature events vary from thirty to one hundred laps. By racing on a half-mile to a mile-and-one-eighth bowl, all the cars are bound to be more or less bunched up. Riding from 70 m.p.h. to 100 m.p.h., drivers naturally must pay close attention, as one false move may spell disaster, and sailing over the top of the bowl is almost a sure trip to the hospital.

Road Racing Unpopular

Racing fans in America prefer this track type of racing to road racing, which has been revived several times but thus far has failed to click with the cash customers.

The majority of cars competing are four-cylinder creations. Miller, Offenhauser, Dryer, Hal, and Hisso motors are the most popular although at least two Curtiss airplane motors will be used as power plants in two cars during 1938.

In September, 1937, Everett Saylor set a

world's record for a half-mile dirt track when he was timed in 22 seconds flat at the Winchester, Indiana, bowl, while all season long, at least eight or ten cars would qualify in 23 seconds on the half-mile banks.

Considering this tremendous speed for such a short distance, one realizes why the C.S.R.A. boasts the fastest circuit in America.

During the past winter and the spring of 1938 many of their tracks have been banked higher and a harder surface of oil spread on the top, which leads many to believe that the boys will be turning in times of 20 seconds before the end of the 1938 season.

Nice 1910. An oil on canvas by Antoine Minartz.

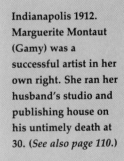

Indianapolis 1912. Marguerite Montaut (Gamy) was a successful artist in her own right. She ran her husband's studio and publishing house on his untimely death at 30. (*See also page 110.*)

107

Maserati, Bugatti and
Auto-Union models
by Rex Hays and
dating from the
thirties.

"The Racers" by
M. Gunst, Austria
c.1906.

After S.C.H.
("Sammy") Davis's
spill at Brooklands in
an Invicta in 1930 his
colleagues presented
him with this F.
Gordon Crosby
bronze.

HETTIN' IT UP

*A Rip-Roarin' Romance of the Raceways,
Written Throughout in Pure (sic!) American by
Kenneth Maxwell*
1936

"Sparkplug" Keohane was up against it, his goat laid a coupla' eggs the day before the big race and pushed most of its buckets thru' the mill.

His only hope was to toon up his old alligator into a gillopy in time to start the next morning. The old clunker was only a flathead with a single stick, four barrels, two pots and not even promoted – however, it took a lot to get Sparkplug down and he went at reconstructing his iron with a will. Luckily he had some lungs that had been previously balanced and a set of special bouncers for his buttons. He slipped a new set of cogs into its rear-end and fitted the larger shoes from his new but now useless goat.

All this took a helluva long time, but with the dawn, after a night of toil, Sparkplug took out his rejuvenated alligator onto the bullring.

After gunning the mill for a few minutes Sparkplug snicked her into foist and let the vice grip. Kicking the mill wide open he aped round a time or two, putting the soup up a bit with each circuit. Sparkplug was the helluva leadfoot, he scorned getting a rope. In the grey light of the early morn he barreled his way round the bullring, paddle flat and the mill arcing.

However, this was Sparkplug's unlucky day. A doughnut blew out and Sparkplug uncorked for a broader. He held her. But another bladder caved, the skin wrapping itself round the shoe and Sparkplug spun into a Gilhooley, eventually draping it on the white stuff.

They took him away in the butcherwagon.
(Thank you, thank you! – Ed., SPEED.)

GLOSSARY

Air out	open up
Alligator	old car
Apeing	going fast
Arcing	peak revs
Barrel	cylinder
Barreling	flat out
Bladder	tyre
Bouncer	valve spring
Bucket	piston
Bullring	dirt track
Butcherwagon	ambulance
Button	valve
Clunker	old car
Cogs	differential
Doughnut	tyre
Drape it on the white stuff	hit the wall
Flathead	side valve engine
Gate	valve
Get a rope	slipstream
Gillopy	car
Gilhooley	uncontrolled slide
Goat	car
Gun the motor	rev up
Iron	car
Kick the mill	open up
Lay an egg	throw a rod
Leadfoot	hard driver
Lung	piston
Mill	engine
Paddle	throttle pedal
Pot	carb.
Promoter	blower
Shoe	wheel
Skin	tyre tread
Soup	speed
Stick	camshaft
Tub	piston
Uncork for a broader	get into a broadside

Heath's racing Panhard fitted with Michelin tyres effortlessly out-paces the "Flying Scotsman" locomotive between Edinburgh and London. The artist Ernest Montaut has been described as the "Father of Automobile Art".

ANOTHER CONTRIBUTION FROM OUR ENTHUSIASTIC AMERICAN FRIEND
By Ted Chase

The major sport of automobile racing has drawn the interest of the public from all sections of the United States for the past 35 years. Some of our foremost men have been vitally interested in the sport, and among the celebrities was Mr. Wm. K. Vanderbilt, Jr., who did more to stimulate interest than any other man of his day. The first available record of his activities is that in August, 1901, when he drove a German Mercedes at Newport, R.I. In 1902, Mr. Vanderbilt went to France and competed in a 570-mile race, but did not finish. In July, 1902, he finished third in a long race at Ardennes, Belgium. He then returned to France and raced in the famous Paris to Madrid event in May, 1903. But again he experienced trouble and failed to finish. A month later he travelled back to Belgium and competed in an important race, but was eliminated. Mr. Vanderbilt then came back to America with his Mercedes car and

astounded the world by driving one mile in 39 seconds, averaging 92 miles an hour on the beach at Daytona, Fla. This was in January, 1904, and there were races every day for a week, and on the closing day, Mr. Vanderbilt won a 50-mile race which was the feature event.

Then came the crowning achievement of his career. He originated the Vanderbilt Cup Race, and made arrangements with Tiffany in New York to make a trophy. This Vanderbilt Cup is at present on exhibit in the National Museum in Washington, D.C. It is 31in. high, holds 101 gallons of liquid and contains 481 ounces of sterling silver.

The first race for this Cup was held on October 8th, 1904, on Long Island, N.Y., being won by George Heath in a French Panhard. Only eleven Vanderbilt Cup races have been held, the last one being at Santa Monica, California, on November 16th, 1916, and was won by the late Dario Resta in a Peugeot. In August, 1933, a revival of the famous road race was held at Elgin, Ill., and proved so popular that there were strong rumours of a revival of the Vanderbilt race, which was planned for the original course on Long Island, but a sanction was not secured.

Mr. Henry Ford had a brief but important part in the early days of racing, and the famous Ford "999" which he built and drove is still in existence, and is in the museum at Dearborn Mich. In October, 1901, Mr. Ford defeated Alexander Winton in a 10-mile match race on the Grosse Point, Mich., dirt track. Mr Ford is still interested in racing, as he has witnessed several 500-mile races on the Indianapolis speedway, and was a referee in one of them. Another very well-known man raced in 1904, it being none other than Mr. John J. Astor. He drove a Mercedes, competing merely for the thrills of the sport. Many of the pioneers of racing are prominent business men to-day, among them being Louis Chevrolet.

The greatest boost and honour for automobile racing has been from the attention and genuine interest shown by many of our Presidents. Presidential interest is the most

powerful advertisement any sport could have. The late Ex-President Wm. H. Taft saw two of the early Vanderbilt races, and the late Ex-President Calvin Coolidge invited Major Segrave for lunch at the White House in Washington, D.C. shortly after Segrave made a new world's record for speed at Daytona. Ex-President Herbert Hoover invited Sir Malcolm Campbell for lunch at the White House in 1931.

Even in Europe great monarchs have shown exceptional enthusiasm in racing, and the ex-Kaiser of Germany saw many events. When Barney Oldfield made 141 m.p.h. at Daytona, Fla., in 1910, the Kaiser sent a personal message congratulating him. Ex-King Alfonso of Spain owned a racing Hispano-Suiza and saw many races held in France, Italy and Spain.

In conclusion, the writer feels that one of the greatest instances where a monarch showed his deep interest in the sport was a reality that has no equal in racing history. On July 4th, 1913, a road race was held between Los Angeles and Sacramento, Calif., and was won by Frank Verbeck in a Fiat. Ed. Waterman in a Buick was second, and Barney Oldfield in a Fiat was third. His Majesty King George of England sent a cablegram to Los Angeles requesting the name of the winner to be cabled back to him.

PLACE TO THE LADIES!
1907

It has hitherto been supposed that the domain of the chauffeur was safe from the encroachments of woman. Those who have entertained this idea, however, must be prepared for a rude shock. We have before us a letter addressed to the Motor Drivers' Employment Agency from a lady, whose name and address, for obvious reasons, it would not be allowable to disclose, seeking employment in this capacity, and setting forth her qualifications. Although a single letter does not prove that the chauffeurs' profession is being "invaded" by the fair sex, any more than one swallow proves that summer has come, yet it

A scarce Omega light box.

must be taken as a sign of the times. Thus, if we project our minds somewhat into the future we shall probably have presented to our imagination a picture not merely of feminine chauffeurs, but of female mechanics and mechanical engineers as well, and mere man will be driven to seek fresh outlets for his powers. To return to the lady in question, we must let her letter speak for itself. She writes in the most matter of fact kind of way, as though there were nothing at all extraordinary in her application, and as though she was not at all conscious of introducing the slightest innovation. Her letter is as follows:

"Sir, I wish to know if you know of anyone who is wanting a lady driver. I am wanting a situation as driver to drive a car. I drove a Darracq for a lady last summer, but this lady is now dead, so I am out of employment. I can also drive a Daimler car. I can do all running repairs, and put tyres on, and am willing to make myself useful. If you know of any lady or elderly couple who are wanting a lady driver, will you please let me know."

111

BMW Commemorative Silver Pewter Cigar box presented to Franz Popp who was responsible for the decision for BMW to manufacture motor cars from 1928. His daughter Erika married the charismatic English driver Richard Seaman in 1938.

This nickelled bronze car mascot was presented to the architect and designer Robert Mallet Stevenson and adorned his Voisin in the 1920s. Jean et Joel Martel leading Art Deco sculptors and silversmiths produced this striking modernist piece in 1925.

A vivid Geo Ham poster for the Montlhèry Autodrome.

The Automobile Club of France sponsored the very first Automotive art exhibition in their headquarters in Paris in 1905. 68 artists were represented.

112

FAMOUS RACING CIRCUITS:
LE MANS, *by T.E. Rose Richards*
LINAS-MONTLHÈRY, *by G.E.T. Eyston*
1935

LE MANS

The Circuit Permanent de la Sarthe is just outside Le Mans, and the route nationale from Tours forms one leg of the course, the remainder having been created from two secondary roads, and by a special road cut by the Automobile Club de l'Ouest. The circuit has a tendency towards an oblong shape, rather than the more usual triangle as at Alessandria.

The grandstands and pits are set near the start of the new road, and, since nearly half the race is run during darkness, special arrangements have been made concerning illumination. The grandstand is a splendid structure, with an enclosure at the front, while the pits are double-tiered – at one time, these were the finest pits in Europe, and they are still the largest on any circuit. Commodious accommodation is necessary in view of the fact that mechanics and attendants have to live in them for twenty-four hours.

From the starting point the road runs under a footbridge into the new-cut highway, traversing a banked bend. The course here is so wide, and with such good surface, that it looks more like part of a specially constructed track than anything else. Some little distance before reaching the Tours highway, the road runs through S-bends, then shoots beneath twin footbridges and corners on to the route nationale.

Immediately after this corner is a short down-grade and a bend to the left, then the road becomes so wide and so straight that it would be hard to duplicate it in the whole of Europe. There is a broad grass verge on either hand, and trees almost completely conceal the buildings forming the little village of Les Hunaudieres. Here is the famous cafe de l'Hippodrome, once a country estaminet, but now an altogether more imposing hostelry which, before the race, is always a meeting place for drivers.

A white line has been drawn down the centre of this splendid straight, as an aid to passing, because cars travel here at extremely high speeds. The stretch is some three miles in length, ending in an easy bend, followed by a deceptive dip which can bring machines unexpectedly fast into the famous Mulsanne corner, where the road turns sharply to the right, between thick pine trees.

The course is much more narrow here and overhanging branches make the road dark. About a mile beyond the corner there is a warning sign which precedes the notorious Arnage Bends. These are S-bends taking their name from a corner just beyond, which is the nearest point to Arnage village. The bends run right, left, then right again, with the actual corner immediately after them; the first of the bends is surfaced partly with broad red bricks, although these are now almost hidden under tar.

When the Arnage turn has been cleared the road remains narrow, with hedges for part of its distance. A series of fast bends ends, just before the grandstand is reached, in White House turn, which has brought grief to many drivers and has been the scene of several multiple smashes. The turn has, however been eased off in recent years while some slight banking has been given to it. From this point, the course returns within the quarter of a mile to the starting point.

Every corner on this circuit carries reflector signs as a warning to drivers at night; most of them are white, but there is usually a red reflector at the actual start of each turn. Sandbanks fronted with wattle fencing protect the spectators, and everything possible has been done to make the course safe.

LINAS-MONTLHÈRY

Just a week after the Le Mans race comes the most famous of all road events: the Grand Prix de l'Automobile Club de France – and it is a little odd that this road race does not take place over a "road" at all. At least, not in the sense that a road event is held over a highway in normal usage.

The course is attached to the Linas-

Montlhèry autodrome, and was specially constructed along the ridge on which the track is set. The circuit commences at the side of the autodrome, diving through a narrow opening on to a tarred road which, at the end of a mile, swings to the left, continues straight for another mile and then dips very abruptly before running into the Couard bends. These consist of a sharp turn, a long curve and another quick bend, with red sandbanks on the right and bushes to the left.

Clear of the "Lacets de Couard", the course drops sharply into a left turn, on the outside of which is a steel control tower erected by the Union Velocipedique de France. Around the turn, the way runs fast and straight down to the Bruyeres hairpin; this, as with all bends, is surfaced with concrete, the remainder of the course being tarred. The run into the hairpin is as beautiful as any point on the circuit, the road being flanked by low gravel banks patched with heather and wild flowers.

After the hairpin comes a short straight, another abrupt bend, then a straight of half a mile, followed by four definite corners which come quickly one after the other and serve to bring cars on to the return road. As a

relief after these corners, the circuit now enters a splendid straight at the far end of which it is possible to see the concrete of the brief climb into the Foret turn. All the way down trees, bushes, heather, low banks of coloured sand and clusters of wild flowers line the road, and through the Foret turn the course swings first to one side and then to another before doubling round the Virage du Gendarme.

The half-mile from Foret to Gendarme corner is usually a rough passage for drivers, because of the way in which the course bends from side to side. Immediately afterwards, however, the road opens into a straight, running parallel with the outer road until it is near the autodrome, when a bend to the left, and another hairpin – Epingle du Faye – brings the circuit back to the track. The course is completed by cars running around the banking at one end, so regaining the starting point opposite the big grandstand.

The course was designed to embrace the best features of a road circuit, and in this it succeeds. The road is adequately wide, and even the most difficult turn looks safe. Although the circuit lacks houses and tele-

Avus track, Germany, popular rendezvous with Berlin motorists during the weekend. Fritz von Opel was the winner at the first meeting held in September 1921.

Renault, founded 1898, were active in racing from the first tentative beginnings of international closed circuit racing in France. The artist is Pierre de Bas.

graph poles, and all those incidental features which add to the spectacular nature of an actual road race, it probably offers a far greater test for men and cars than any natural course could possibly achieve.

An Exclusive Interview With Herr Reiners
Director of the Avus Track

The construction of a new road has necessitated the rebuilding of the north turn of the famous Avus track. Improvements which, it is believed, will raise even higher the already colossal speeds for which the Avus is deservedly famous. Picture a wall of earth over 60 feet high, stretching round in a semi-circle, with about 200 yards between the open ends. The inner face is banked with clinkerbricks, and has a slope of almost 1 in 1. Introduce a low, streamlined racing car into the picture, skirling round the turn at 125 m.p.h. or more. That is what the new North Turn at the Avus Track, Berlin, is like.

World's fastest

Not content with building the fastest roads for ordinary motor traffic Germany will now possess easily the fastest racing track in the world, when the latest modifications are complete.

Having had a glimpse of the new turn, I was anxious to hear what Herr Hellmuth Reiners, the director of the Avus, and leader of the Berlin Brandenburg section of the D.D.A.C., planned for the forthcoming season.

"When will the modifications to the track be complete?" I asked him.

"About the end of March", he replied, glancing out of his window, from which the towering mound of earth was clearly visible. "The old turn, which was banked at an angle of only 1 in 10, used to run just outside this office. But a new road had to be built, leading to the Exhibition buildings" – the Motor Show was in progress at the time – "and so the Berlin Corporation has compensated us for the building of a new turn".

"The Avus is run by a private company, is it not?" I asked.

"Yes," said Herr Reiners, "the track was begun in 1913, but work was interrupted by the War. It was recommenced in 1919, and finished in September, 1921. We had a two-days' programme of racing for the opening ceremony."

"What does 'Avus' mean?" I said. "The letters A.V.U.S. stand for Automobil Verkehrs und Ubungs Strasse, which in English would mean, literally, "Automobile Traffic and Practice Street". It is not by any means

By the 1920s Réné Lalique was specialising in glass. Here are two excellent examples of the period – a Pintade and Frog.

only a racing track, as you probably know. It is used very considerably as a tollroad from Berlin to Wannsee and Potsdam".

100 m.p.h. with ease

Before seeing Herr Reiners I had been round the track in the latest 5.4-litre supercharged Mercedes-Benz. We could not take the new turn, as the approaches to the banking were not then complete, but the car was able to maintain 100 m.p.h. with perfect ease all along the two parallel straights. The Avus, it may be mentioned, consists of two parallel one-way roads, practically straight, and joined by a bend at either end.

"What difference to the length of the track has the new turn made?" I asked Herr Reiners.

"We have not yet had it surveyed, but the difference will not be great. Formerly it was 19.573 kilometres (just over 12 miles), and I think now it will be about 19.3 kilometres.

"The fastest lap on the old circuit was at 162 m.p.h. by Stuck with his Auto-Union, in 1935, and in that year, before the new work was begun, Fagioli won the Avusrennen for Mercedes-Benz at 148 m.p.h. over 150 miles."

Angle of banking

"What is the angle of the banking at the south turn?" I said, marvelling at such speeds.

"The south turn, which is not being altered, is banked at 1 in 9. The surface there is tar-concrete. The new north turn, which has special non-skid clinker-bricks, is banked at 43° or nearly 1 in 1, with a radius of 92.6 metres. The banking is not concave, and the 43° slope is maintained over a width of 12 metres, to give ample room for passing. At about 11 metres from the top the track is sloped at 75-80°, or nearly vertical, to form a retaining wall. Then, as you have seen, there is a narrow strip at the bottom, which is quite flat. The total width, from edge to edge, is 22 metres."

Method of construction

This method of construction for the banking is indeed interesting. At Brooklands, for instance, the steepest part at the top of the banking, where cars can maintain their highest speed, is narrow. Thus, if one of the fastest cars wishes to pass a machine only slightly slower, the driver of the latter has to pull down, and probably slacken speed. At the new Avus turn a car at the bottom will be able to travel as fast as a car at the top.

Free formula

To a question about the forthcoming Avus-rennen in May, Herr Reiners replied that there would be two heats and a final, as in 1935, and the whole meeting would be run under "free formula." This means that the Grand Prix formula weight limit will not apply, so that such cars as Caracciola's record-

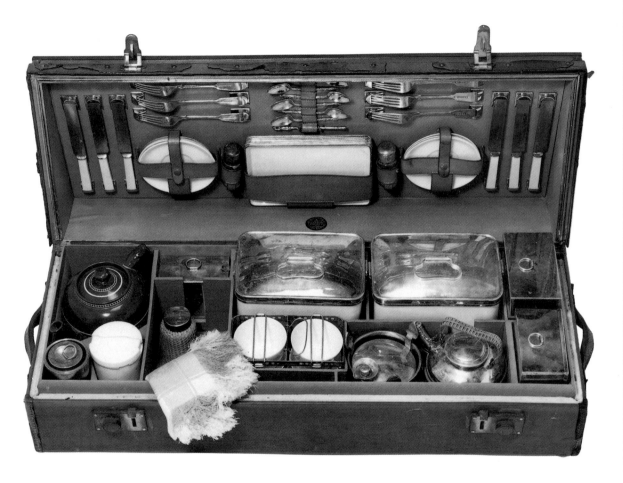

A Finnigan's leather bound trunk for six. The correct equipment for picknicking.

breaking Mercedes-Benz will be eligible.

"What is that building in course of construction which I saw over the rim of the banking?" I asked.

"That is the new offices of the Avus Syndicate", replied Herr Reiners. "It will also include a restaurant, and an official stand for the races. But a new grandstand, to hold 4,500 people, is being built just at the end of the turn. It is nearly finished, as I expect you saw."

Valuable data

Herr Reiners, who is a recognised authority on road construction, went on to say that valuable data had been established from the methods used in the construction of the Avus

for the building of the reichsautobahnen, or special motor roads.

Mention must certainly be made of Stuck's remarkable 101.56 m.p.h. record for the standing kilometre, which was accomplished at the Avus. Wheel grip for the terrific acceleration involved must have been considerably aided by the special surface, for which it was discovered that a grain of 10 mm. was best in aiding adhesion, instead of 30 mm., as previously favoured.

"Speeds on the Avus have always been double those on the ordinary road", said Herr Reiners proudly, and, indeed, if one works it out, that is the case. The speed of the fastest touring cars is approximately half that of the Grand Prix machines.

Réné Lalique car
mascot.

Sites For Record Breaking
By Eric Sydney

The ideal course for record breaking, for distances over ten miles, would be perfectly circular, with continuous banking for the whole circumference, the slope of the banking being so graduated as to give "normal" reaction, perpendicular to the surface of the track, at all speeds likely to be encountered.

In order to reduce the stresses on car, driver and track to the minimum, and to approximate as closely as possible to ordinary flat road use, the track should be as large in radius (or long in lap) as possible.

The above ideal has never yet been attained. Owing to the cost of banking construction, the usual design has been that of banked ends, joined by unbanked straights. For such a design to be successful it appears, at first sight, that the straights should be as long as possible, in order that the minimum number of changes from flat to banking shall be encountered in a given time or distance. Various considerations have, however, led to most of the world's tracks being fairly "square" in shape, with relatively short straights (e.g., Brooklands, Montlhèry, Indianapolis). The chief of these considerations are those of land available, servicing, control and visibility from grandstands, all of which favour a compact layout for the course.

All tracks may, therefore, be regarded as approximating to one or other of these two ideals:–

a. Circular fully-banked tracks.

b. Tracks with long straights joined by fully-banked curves at the ends.

Reviewing the various tracks which appear in the list of records, we find the following position.

Brooklands

The world's veteran speedway is still used occasionally for records, but its design does not make it suitable for the highest modern speeds. Lately, the only world's records which have been set up there have been the standing start mile and kilo "acceleration records", which were held by John Cobb, Napier Railton, and Raymond Mays, E.R.A. These records were subsequently annexed by the German "Formula" cars, and it is doubtful whether it will ever be possible to regain them at Brooklands. A large number of "class" records, however, taken at Brooklands, are still on the International list.

Montlhèry

This amazing speed track is still the scene of great activity, but as speeds rise higher and higher the difficulties of driving on this short-lap track become greater and greater.

At present, however, all the world's records for distances greater than 5,000 kilos, or 24-hours, are held at Montlhèry.

Atlantic City, U.S.A.

Although the fast board track at Atlantic City closed down some years ago, owing to financial difficulties, it is still represented in the list of International Class records, by a group of Studebaker records in Class "B", set up in 1928.

The track was much used in its day, speeds up to 150 m.p.h. being attained on its steep banking.

Turning to other possible sites for record attempts, we find that in addition to Daytona Beach U.S.A., and "Ninety Mile" Beach, New Zealand, which are only suitable for short-distance "straightaway" records, there still remain a few places where conditions are more favourable to high speeds over long distances. The first of these is the makeshift Avus track, and the remainder are natural sites.

The Avus, Berlin

This track is ordinarily a five-mile toll road, which has been made into a two-lane road by dividing a broad avenue by means of a central grass strip.

In order to make a closed circuit for racing, slightly banked curves have been constructed at each end, giving a total lap of 12.2 miles. If these curves were fully banked the track would satisfy the ideal condition, (b) above. Actually, the curves can only be taken at 60 to 80 m.p.h., but even so the possibilities of the track are considerable, as the following achievements indicate:

"The Right Crowd and no Crowding" was the slogan of the BARC. Here is a typical Paddock scene at Brooklands. An ERA club meeting in the thirties.

119

1933. Czaikowski, World's HourRecord, 132 m.p.h.

1934. Von Stuck, World's Hour Record, 134 m.p.h.

1934. Von Stuck, 100 kilo Record, 155 m.p.h.

1933. 200 mile race. Winner's speed, 128 m.p.h.

1934. 200 mile race, in rain. Speed, 127 m.p.h.

1935. 120 mile race. Speed, 148 m.p.h.

This track, with its long straights permitting of sustained high speeds, and its relatively short banking, is attracting more and more attention.

A remarkable achievement, early in 1935, was the record run by Schweder and Hasse, with an Adler car, in which a group of class records, from 400 kilos to six days, were broken at over 68 m.p.h., with ordinary traffic running on the toll road. A further run was made in November with a 1,500 c.c. streamlined saloon, in which a mean speed of 76 m.p.h. was maintained for 96 hours.

The other venues for record attempts of the future are natural sites where a circular course of long lap-distance can be laid out on flat ground. The three most interesting are:–

a. Salduro (Bonneville) Salt Bed, Utah, U.S.A.

b. Muroc dry lake, California,

c. Verneuk Pan dry lake, South Africa.

Details of these natural tracks, and of the records established on them, are given below.

Conditions on these courses can be made to approach very closely to the ideal conditions of a circular banked track, the size of the lap being made so great that the angle of the banking theoretically required becomes small enough to be almost neglected.

Bonneville Salt Bed, Salduro, Wendover, Utah, U.S.A.

This bed is the remains of a salt lake, which dries out completely between June and October, each year, leaving a hard surface of salt. The site is 125 miles west of Salt Lake City, and is 4,200ft. above sea level.

American record attempts have taken place at Bonneville for several years, with results enumerated below, while 1935 has seen two successful British long-distance efforts there, and has also seen Sir Malcolm Campbell attain his life's ambition, with a world's land speed record of over 300 m.p.h., on a straight-away on the salt bed.

The possibilities of the site have not been entirely explored but an area of approximately 8 miles by 12 is available and a 20-mile circle or a 30-mile oval can be readily laid out.

For 24-hour record runs, two courses, one of 10 miles lap and one of 121 miles, are marked out in the salt by the A.A.A. surveyors. The car is then run on the 10-mile circuit, until serious damage of the surface appears, when it is switched over to the longer circuit.

The first effort at Salduro to attract attention was carried out by the Pierce-Arrow Co. in 1932, when Ab Jenkins, himself a native of Salt Lake City, accomplished a run of 12 hours at 112 m.p.h., setting up many new American records.

In 1933 they made a further effort, culminating in an amazing single-handed run by Jenkins, who established records from 500 kilos at 124 m.p.h. to 24 hours at 117 m.p.h. After considerable delay, these records were submitted to the A.I.A.C.R., and homologated as world's records.

In 1934 Jenkins again made a successful single-handed run, taking fifteen world's records at speeds between 132 m.p.h. for 500 kilos and 127 m.p.h. for the 24 hours. The car is described as a Jenkins-Special, believed to be of Auburn origin.

Last year saw considerable activity at Bonneville. In June, Jenkins took the world's coveted hour record at 143 m.p.h., In July, John Cobb with his Napier-Railton made a clean sweep of all records from 50 kilos at 154 m.p.h., and the hour at 151 m.p.h. to the 24 hours at 134.7 m.p.h.

In August, Jenkins and Gulotta, with a Duesenberg, retook the hour and the 24-hour records, by the narrowest of margins at 152.1 and 135.4 m.p.h. respectively.

September saw Captain G. E. T. Eyston out

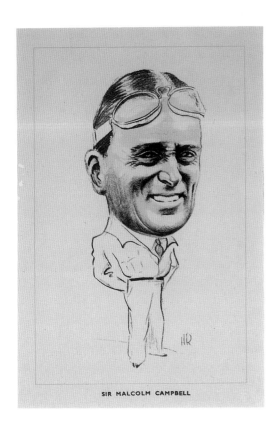

SIR MALCOLM CAMPBELL

G. E. T. EYSTON

Count Czaikowski's record breaking "Bug".

Speed Kings. Sir Malcolm Campbell of "Bluebird" fame and George Eyston, professional records man and fine engineer.

121

"By Appointment to his late Majesty King Edward VII". Ceramic panel from Michelin House, the London headquarters of the Clermont-Ferrand tyre firm.

on the salt bed, with his new Rolls-Royce engined car, "Speed of the Wind". With this machine he took the world's ten-mile record at 167 m.p.h., after it had stood to the credit of the Australian "Wizard Smith" since 1932, and then proceeded to take the hour record at 159 m.p.h. and the 24-hour record at 140.5 m.p.h.

As already mentioned, Sir Malcolm Campbell also visited the salt bed in August, and achieved a new world's speed record at 301 m.p.h., an increase of over 24 m.p.h. on his previous record.

Two "stock car" efforts may also be mentioned.

In 1934, a Chrysler "Airflow" saloon set up a new American record for "closed stock cars", averaging 84 m.p.h. for 24 hours. In 1935, an Auburn car established a "stock car" record of five hours' non-stop at over 100 m.p.h.

Muroc Dry Lake, California, U.S.A.

This course, in the remote desert flats of California, has only been used to a limited extent, and information about it is scanty. The surface is baked mud and it is reasonably flat, but covered with a network of small cracks.

The first record to show the world the possibilities of this site was an astonishing 1,500 c.c. mile record at 164 m.p.h. by the late Frank Lockhart, in 1927, with a special supercharged Miller car. This still stands as a class record.

From 1927 to 1933 the inaccessibility of the site led to the abandonment of further efforts there, but in 1933 two cars were taken out and Muroc appeared again in the record list.

With a 5-litre "Union Special", Fred Frame set up world's records for 50 miles and 50 kilos at 136 and 139 m.p.h., while Harry Hartz broke the short distance Class "C" records with the same car, at speeds between 151 m.p.h. for one mile and 146 m.p.h. for ten miles. These records were subsequently taken by Von Stuck at Avus.

Class "B", 8-litre records, were taken by an Auburn, driven by H. Wilcox, "Howdy" of that ilk, the speeds ranging from 200 miles at 113 m.p.h. to 12 hours at 105 m.p.h. All these records were subsequently taken by Jenkins at Bonneville.

Verneuk Pan, South Africa

This dried-up lake is similar to Muroc. The area available is 37 by 17 square miles. Its chief disadvantages are its remoteness from civilisation and the absence of approach roads. The site is 450 miles from Cape Town, 420 miles from the nearest railhead and 2,000 feet above sea-level.

The surface is baked mud, the rainfall being only 1-inch in four years, but this surface is covered with ridges of sharp pebbles, 200-300 yards apart, which have to be cleared by native labour.

During the hours of sunlight the Pan becomes veiled with heat haze and deceptive mirages make the observation of mark-flags difficult; for this reason record attempts there are better made at the crack of dawn.

Two record attempts have taken place at Verneuk, the more important being Sir Malcolm Campbell's 1929 expedition, when speeds up to 218 m.p.h. were recorded over distances up to 10 kilometres. All of these records have since been broken many times by Sir Malcolm himself.

Earlier in 1929 a young South African, driving a De Soto, set up a South African 24-hour record at 62.7 m.p.h., the run being made on a 7-mile circuit, which was covered over 200 times.

A line of cars rushing up the finishing straight at Brooklands by the French race-horse painter Vallet. The painting was used for official race cards and shows Daimler, de Dietrich, Napier, Mors and Renault.

BEFORE YOU RACE AT BROOKLANDS
S C H Davis, 1936

Brooklands is an interesting and amusing place, but it also has its serious side. Therefore, remember that the mere fact of becoming a racing driver does not absolve any man from using his intelligence.

Before starting, remember certain simple things; for example, the flag signals, because neglect of these may lead to a crash. Briefly, the flags used are light blue, dark blue, black, green, yellow, and black and white chequered. The light blue means "keep lower, someone else wants to pass", the dark blue means "be cautious, someone has crashed", all the other flags mean "stop", the yellow flag "stop instantly."

If you are travelling at 90 m.p.h. and a bee is travelling at 10 m.p.h., if the bee hits your eye there will be trouble. This we do not mind, except that you may run into someone else – therefore wear goggles always.

More people have got into difficulties through not being comfortable and secure in the driving seat with all controls easy to get at, than from almost anything else.

Racing wheels are necessary because the others collapse.

A car will run wild or be docile at any speed, according to whether the shock absorbers are loose or tight, and the tyre pressures even and sufficient.

Leaving the Paddock by the wrong gate frequently leads to end-on collisions.

Entering the Paddock by the wrong gate does so as well.

As you turn on to the Home Banking you will see a black line. Keep on the near side of this, the far side is reserved for cars that are going very quickly.

Make all adjustments in a bay.

If you leave the bay without looking round, you may be hit by a motor cycle doing 100, and it will be your fault.

All round the Track, 50 feet from the inner edge, there is a dotted black line. Theoretically, this is the 60 m.p.h. line, actually a car lapping at 90 can be held on.

At the Fork there are two important lines which commence at the end of the Byfleet Banking. One of these is black, near the outer edge of the Track; the other is bright blue. If your lap speed does not exceed 100 m.p.h. you must keep on the near side of the blue line. Cars differ, but it is possible to lap at a speed of 105 m.p.h., keeping the car six feet on the near side of the blue line and to hold it there with one hand.

Always hold the car a little lower on the banking than the position it naturally wants to take, otherwise you will baulk other people, which is not fair.

If you find difficulty in keeping on the near side of the blue line, try to come off the Byfleet Banking in a gradual curve earlier and aim for the centre of the Track just after the Cobham River Bridge. Follow the blue line curve accurately, and always, if you can, leave room for another car to pass between yours and the blue line.

Follow the blue line curve accurately, and always, if you can, leave room for another car to pass between yours and the blue line.

If the car is lapping at over 100 m.p.h., you will not be asked to keep it on the near side of the blue line.

In that case do not cross the black line or you will be run into from astern by a very fast car, and it will be your fault.

Take the car on to the Home Banking and the Byfleet Banking a little higher than its normal position, then come down to normal. The car will probably swerve downwards, for which you must be prepared.

Keep as far as you can away from the dotted black line 10 feet from the top of the banking.

When you come out from behind the Members' Hill, remember that with certain directions of the wind the car will be blown up the banking, and be prepared to hold it in its proper place.

Whatever happens, do not swerve sharply or apply the brakes vigorously when the car is going fast. Observe carefully the course of cars ahead and try to anticipate their movements.

Be prepared for other cars passing on either

Roy Nockolds' study shows Jack Dunfee's consistently successful 1921 Ballot on the Member's or "Home" banking at Brooklands track in Surrey.

side of you. You can hear them coming from astern, and you can glance round or use your mirror, especially on the Railway Straight, where you can tell whether a faster car is coming and judge when it will pass.

When you are on the banking, if a faster car passes lower down, that implies a hint that you are driving too high.

Half the trouble that occurs when a tyre bursts is due to the driver being startled, so don't be.

If a car or tyre bursts, do not swerve suddenly to the inner edge of the Track. Look round first to make sure no other car is coming.

In mountain racing pass on the outside at Chronograph Villa turn, on either side at the Members' Bridge turn, but do not cut across the path of another car as you take the Members' Bridge turn.

A thoroughly dirty car or driver is generally inefficient.

Smoking in a racing car is heavily frowned upon.

Do not grouse at every difficulty; motor racing would be quite dull if there were no difficulties.

If a large column of black smoke is seen coming from some portion of the Track, the deduction should be that a car is on fire, and therefore that a fire engine or a number of people with extinguishers may be crossing the Track to that fire. Don't expect, therefore, to find the Track absolutely clear.

At the top of the Home Banking, at a point close to the parapet of the bridge and just before the banking slopes down to the Railway Straight, there is a bad bump. On leaving the Home Banking, no matter at what speed, don't tackle this bump, but pull the car off the banking early so that it is not within ten feet of the outer edge at this point.

POLICE TRAPS AND THE COMING SUMMER –
HOW TO MEET THE ENEMY
1907

It is true that the members of the Automobile Association are well covered and warned by the active and intelligent scouts employed by that organisation to perform the work of safeguarding the public as it should be performed by those public servants, the police. It is clearly impossible for the A.A., feverishly energetic as it is, to guard all the points on all the roads the police regard as perilous, though it were a hundred fold richer and stronger than it is. By information which has reached us from time to time it is evident that during the coming summer the police persecution of motorists is to be pursued with inquisitorial ferocity. Police traps are to be multiplied ad nauseam, and to be worked over long distances, electrically and by day and night. There is a suggestion that any speed over eight miles per hour after dark is in one particular quarter to be regarded as dangerous and will expose drivers to legal proceedings. Now this is persecution, organised intentional persecution, without qualification, and must be resisted to the uttermost, unless motorists submit to being hounded off the roads altogether. The mutual consideration and support which marked the motoring spirit in the early days must return for the purposes of self-preservation against this systematised persecution. If motorists could hope for anything approaching a reasonable administration of justice, or even a rational apportionment of punishment for purely technical breaches of an absurd law, there would be no need for such measures as we propose.

If the avowed intention of making certain sections of the roads of this country impossible to the pioneers of the traffic of the future is to be combated, then steps must be taken at once and concerted action resolved upon. Upon first thoughts our suggestion may be regarded as Quixotic, but, after all, it is only urged in the interests of our liberties upon the road. If motorists would agree to what we

propose they would win triumphantly before this year was out, though we are fain to admit that rigid compliance with our suggestion would mean much grit, self-denial, and at times no little inconvenience to those concerned.

Briefly, the idea is that, at all costs, and at all inconveniences, a motorist stopped in a police trap, in lieu of proceeding after compliance with the requests of the officers concerned, should return on his tracks to a suitable point short of the trap and there await the arrival of the next car. The newcomer would be stopped, put into possession of the facts, and would then, on his part, and as tribute for his salvation, halt until the next car came along, when he in his turn should be free to proceed. Such procedure is perfectly within a motorist's rights. The police have had a shot at showing such action to be illegal, but were

Studies by F. Gordon Crosby a remarkably versatile and prolific artist working in pen and ink, pen and wash, Conte crayon and watercolour. Crosby received no formal training but proved an especially gifted illustrator, evoking the power and speed of the Golden era.

worsted before the Lord Chief Justice, and are not likely to try again. Such mutual self-help, loyally carried out, is always the resource of persecuted sections of the community, and if an unwritten compact of the kind were loyally observed by motorists wherever necessary, these mean snares, instituted by the police at the instance of money-grabbing councils and benches, would very shortly become extinct. We are aware the proposal has a Utopian ring, but adopted with enthusiasm all over the country, as motorists should adopt it, and generously observed, the inconveniences so incurred, though admittedly onerous at first, would not long be necessary. If anything of the kind is to be done, we have no hesitation in saying that Colonel Bosworth and Stenson Cooke, with their Association at their back, should be the evangelists of this gospel of self-help.

MOTORING IN CALIFORNIA
Cars, Gasolene, and Hot Sandwiches!
By Ella Winter 1928

America is probably the easiest country in the world to motor in, and California the easiest State in America. In contrast to Italy, everything is done for the motorist's convenience, and not for that of the authorities.

The most striking difference is in railway crossings. In France and Italy gates are kept closed while the motorist honks himself hoarse; between Genoa and Rapallo is a crossing which always keeps one waiting twenty minutes. It almost ended the Genoa Peace Conference, when the Russian delegates at Rapallo, unpunctual at best, had to add this twenty minutes to their lateness.

In America there are no gates at all, no death's head and cross bones to warn the

driver, but a red signal which swings to and fro when a train is near. I have not once seen cars lined up to a railway crossing, in six months in California.

Further to aid the motoring traveller are an infinite number of service stations painted in flaring colours, red and orange, red, white and blue, all yellow or all red. They have mechanical pumps with eight or ten different brands of gasolene, mechanical pumps for water and air. The boys at these service stations are picked for their friendliness, cheerfulness and courtesy, and they almost take the place of policemen in their warnings and their ability to give directions. At any rate they are a great deal easier to locate than a policeman, for there are many more of them. They check your oil and wipe off your windshield without the asking, and sometimes dust the whole car, if you have the time to wait. One man, who gave me petrol between Gonzales and Soledad, 7,000 miles from England, asked me what part of the Empire I came from. I sounded as if I might be Australian, he said. "I am", I exclaimed, surprised, "though I have lived the last seventeen years in London". "I lived there eight years", he replied, his eyes shining, "but my home is in Bristol. I went home last year hoping to stay, but my Californian wife couldn't stand the climate. So here I am again – homesick in the Californian desert".

Some Service Stations have restaurants attached, rooms for dancing and recreation, and some even sleeping apartments. They advertise "Ice Cold Drinks", "Eat Here", "Barbecued Dinner", "Hot Sandwiches," and one little town, Holy City, some eighty miles south of San Francisco, has a large painting of heaven, complete with stars, angels and wings, and advertise "Agreeable Dancing is as near Heaven as you will ever get. Stop Here."

Eating on the road provides many thrills. You can take your own food and picnic on the side of a canyon, with soft yellow hills hiding mountain lions, coyotes, deer, wild cats or skunks, opposite you; you can stop at an hotel or restaurant or inn; at an auto camp or a fruit stall; or at a little shack in which a chef with a white cap will cook you "hot dogs" (Frankfurter sausages on a sandwich) or chili and beans or a hot roast beef sandwich. One such place advertised "Meats cooked by oakwood", and they told us that meant less flame, and therefore the "barbecued" sandwiches would not taste smoky.

Though the speed limit all over California is forty miles, many motorists manage fifty, sixty or seventy with ease. There are no police traps (they are legally forbidden!), but cops come up on motor-bicycles or in roadsters, pace you, blow their whistles and stop you if you are exceeding the limit. Fines vary from five to fifty dollars according to your offence, your behaviour, and how you talk to the Judge. One woman who called a cop "monkey face" said that satisfaction cost her twenty dollars. The smooth, wide, level roads and long distances are a sore temptation to speeding, but the temptation is offset by the scenery of California, of which one can never see enough.

Auto-illustration by Ranson for *Die Dame* who published a motoring number every year to coincide with the Berlin Motor Show.

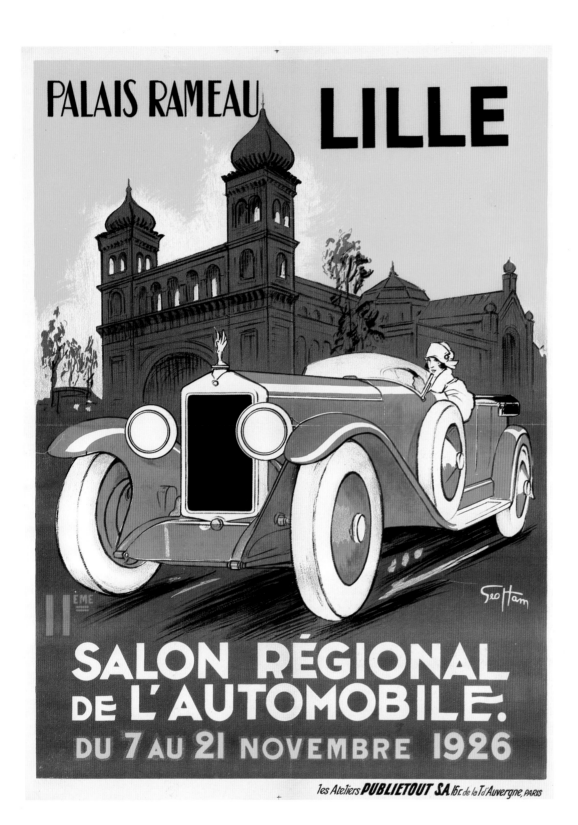

A Lille Salon poster by Geo. Ham.

ICE! SOME MONTE CARLO RALLY IMPRESSIONS
By H. K. Hardy 1936

Of all the events with which the sporting calendar is congested, the Monte Carlo Rally is undoubtedly one of the very finest. Modern Grand Prix racing, magnificent sport though it may be, is only for the fortunate few, but the Rally is open to the ordinary enthusiast with its own special advantages and peculiar appeal.

Few people seem to realise exactly what the Rally involves for those who start from the remoter points, and are apt to liken it to an enormously lengthy and monotonous Continental edition of the R.A.C. Rally. Actually the difficulties are far greater than those ever experienced in this country, and questions of languages, fatigue, temperament and weather have always to be met, apart from the problems of finding the route in unfamiliar countries, problems which invariably arise late at night and far from any human habitation. Often there is no alternative to a road impassable from snow or flood, garages and even petrol supplies are few and far between, and as for spares the competitor has to rely entirely upon those which can be carried in the car.

If the weather conditions are bad enough to cause delay, the unfortunate competitor has to struggle along as best he can with little or no time to spare for proper meals or rest, eking out the intervals with coffee from a flask, sandwiches and fruit, and it is quite usual for competitors to run throughout the Rally without seeing a bed at all. Blizzards sometimes block the routes for days at a time, and hardly a year passes without it proving impossible to cover at least one route within the time allowed. It is only necessary to compare the lists of starters and finishers to get an idea of the extraordinary obstacles encountered on certain routes.

Although such discomforts may not suit everyone's taste, they are all a part of the game, and such difficulties lend a spice of risk to the run which seems to be one of the few adventures left in civilised Europe to-day.

At times the long trek can be very monotonous, especially in the South of France where, with the journey almost completed, the car races down the long straight tree-lined roads in a desperate endeavour to make up time. The white-washed tree trunks on these roads have a curiously mesmeric effect as they flit past one's tired eyes, making it hard to avoid dropping off to sleep.

At other times it is a long struggle against adversity; the car may be miles off the correct route, trouble may occur with the chains or electrical system, perhaps a leaking tank or radiator, a tired-out crew, or snow, ice or fog, any of these can be the cause of serious delay, and ice is probably the worst of the lot.

On one recent Rally, when coming South from Umea, a hard frost, following a thaw, covered the roads with a sheet of black ice inches thick, and that night was one of terrific tension – the driver perspiring with anxiety – the car slewing from side to side of the narrow ribbon of ice which was the road to Stockholm.

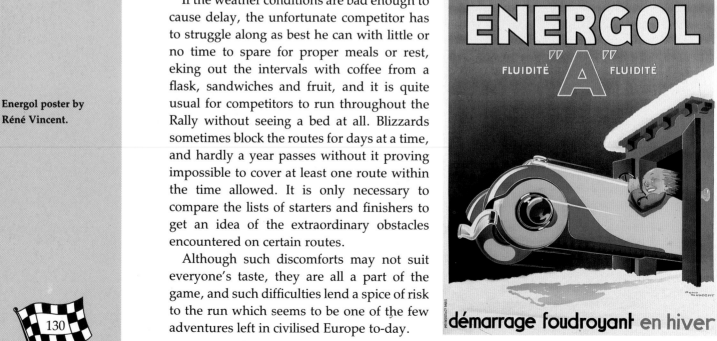

Energol poster by Réné Vincent.

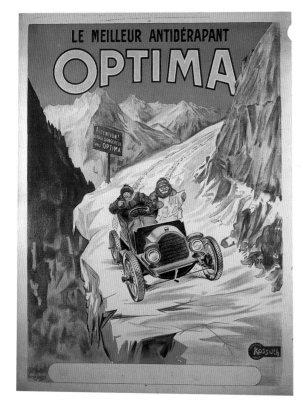

Picture to yourself the scene. It is late on a January afternoon, and the low-built "4½" is cruising silently along a lonely snow-bound road through the heart of a dense forest. The trees with their branches bending under the weight of a heavy fall of snow, are so close that they overhang the road. There is no wind and no sound but the low boom of the exhaust and the pleasant chink of the chain-shod rear wheels on the frozen snow. For many miles there have been no signs of life, not even a forester's hut, and a few tyre tracks are the only indications of the twentieth century. The light is failing fast and the others are sprawling back in their seats dozing uneasily. Soon the headlamps are needed, and at once the scene alters. The frozen snow glistens attractively, the trees seem to grow thicker and darker, and the road itself narrows strangely, giving the effect of a tunnel through the forest.

Once or twice a belated local car is passed, otherwise the road seems completely deserted. Oil gauge and ammeter receive frequent glances, speedometer and route card

131

Alfred Neubauer (*far right*). As racing manager of Mercedes, he had no equal in the history of motor racing.

show that we should be in excellent time at Stockholm, and time is whiled away in pleasant anticipation of the hot meal and blazing fire that await us in that distant capital.

We run on thus for an hour or two, the road winding monotonously through the forest. Occasionally, when rounding a bend, a fleeting glimpse of a tail-lamp far ahead shows the presence of another car, a competitor perhaps, and one speculates idly upon his identity.

On each side of the road a deep ditch is concealed by a bank thrown up by the snow plough, and these banks must be avoided at all costs, for if a front wheel is allowed to touch the bank it will instantly dig right in and send the car into the ditch. Since assistance is hard to come by in the wilds, the situation might easily be serious. As night draws on, the surface is beginning to get slippery and caution is needed. The road gradually changes to a darker colour and the car seems to slide a trifle on the corners. Care is needed with the controls, and too heavy a touch sets the tail wagging ominously. The steering becomes strangely light, and, finally, the eccentric motion arouses the others; the "Skipper" decides to take over and we pause to fit chains to the front wheels. Fitting the chains in the dark is easier said than done, the road is a sheet of steeply cambered black ice and it is actually impossible to stand upright without clinging to the car for support. We even have to cut a hole in the ice for the base of the jack! The ice is literally inches thick, and after a wretched struggle with chains that are always just too long or just too short we gingerly slither round to the door and start off again hopefully. Steering is greatly improved by the chains, but the surface is far too treacherous at anything more than 15 or 20 m.p.h., and we are supposed to average 25!

Conditions become steadily worse, the car waltzes in the most astounding manner and time and again slews almost broadside across the road. It seems inconceivable that we can keep out of the ditch, and once in the ditch our chances of success would almost certainly be ruined.

The slightest touch on brake or throttle sends the car sliding alarmingly, with the "Skipper" fighting desperately for control. The tension is terrific and the perspiration is literally streaming down his face, although the temperature is well below freezing point. We lean forward fascinated by the snow banks – waiting, waiting for the car to gyrate wildly across the road and into that fatal ditch.

Once the car gets off the crown of the road it is almost impossible to coax it back again, and it slowly crabs down into the edge of the bank. The steering is completely useless and twice we have to get out, and, standing thigh deep in the bank, we actually push the car bodily up the camber again !

Here and there great scars in the banks bear witness to the flounderings of other cars, and, in one place, we stop to help the crew of a ditched car which blocks the road. United efforts drag it out, and our own car is warily edged past. The other driver tries in vain to get away from the side of the road, his car merely crabs hopelessly, and we push it up the camber as if it were mounted on skates. Twice we meet cars travelling in the opposite direction which stop on the very crown of the road, their drivers not daring to move an inch down the camber, so, while the "Skipper" edges gingerly past, we stand in the snow

again and keep the car from sliding too far down.

For mile after mile we hardly dare speak, obsessed with the thought that our attempt, carefully planned so many weeks ahead might end in disaster at literally any moment. Stockholm, once so near, seems impossibly remote, we can never reach the control on time. Conditions are hopeless, even the few pedestrians in the scattered hamlets we pass can only make progress by clinging on to trees and fences. So it goes on for seventy or eighty miles; often we pass abandoned cars and lorries in the ditch, sometimes a competitor who had given up the struggle as hopeless. But just when things are at their very worst we suddenly run off the ice on to frozen snow again, and the last few miles into the city come as an absolute relief.

It is experiences such as this which give the Rally its peculiar fascination, and which bring the same competitors together year after year. The thrills, the difficulties, the feeling of struggling against hopeless odds, the weariness, the long lonely roads in strange lands, the determination to fight sleep when the crew is tired out, the elation as the car races along the Corniche road into Monte Carlo after four days and nights on the road, all go to blend the Rally into one of the finest adventures that the enthusiast could wish for.

Edwardian plates by Sarreguemines. China plates proved an inexpensive way to exploit the image of the motor car and were often produced by the smaller potteries.

Royal Doulton of Burslem, England were widely known for the production of one of the finest industrial glazes in Europe. Doulton pieces were popular in France, Germany and the U.S. as well as the home market.

133

Shell advertising from Réné Vincent.

Death Crashes Without Tears

In the early days of the film, fakes were so common that to-day many people imagine that many thrilling scenes depicted are not quite what they seem.

When Reg Kavanagh realised this he set to work to alter things.

Reg was a dirt-track rider, who had been a boxer and racing car driver. While lying in hospital, having broken his arm, he decided to form a crash squad which would be willing to stage real crashes for British films.

At the moment the crash squad consists of Reg, as leader, and eight dare-devils who are experts in car and motor-cycle crashing, aeroplane crashing, aeroplane wing walking and all sorts of death-defying feats.

When a crash is wanted for a film, the squad is ready, and the resultant crash is a real one without any faking.

Thus, in the film "Bulldog Jack", Reg did a 65 miles per hour head-on crash with a Bentley car, and in the film "The Crouching

Beast", he deliberately drove a 40-horse-power Daimler car in a 45 m.p.h. crash and turnover.

In a recent film, "No Limit", which deals with the famous motor-cycle T.T. races in the Isle of Man, the squad do some breathtaking high-speed riding stunts and crashes, and here Reg broke his right arm for the ninth time.

I asked him how he did the crashes and he laughed.

"It is quite easy. You simply prepare for the crash, jump clear, and that is all. When you have crashed as many times as I have, you learn what to expect, and whether it is motor-cycle, motor car or aeroplane crashing, all you need is quick thinking."

This sounds so simple, but I know that Reg feels an inward qualm every time he steps off an aeroplane with a parachute, even though he has made the descent 237 times, and he remembers that the first squad he organised went to the Continent and Reg was the only one to return alive and uninjured, and that when the second squad went to Germany

Geneva Salon poster

The automobile Salons held at Moscow and St. Petersburg were Society occasions. Before the Great War Russia was a customer for the "Voitures de Luxe" with high society taking its lead from the Royal Family and the Tsar.

three of the dare-devils were killed in the first week.

A few weeks ago he and his squad staged some head-on crashes at Manchester to prove that crashes are not faked, and thousands of people saw two high-powered cars crash head-on, become total wrecks, and catch fire, while Reg came out with a split nose and head and a shoulder out of joint.

For filming purposes he says "The difficulty is to arrange that the crash happens right in the camera's eye. Unless that can be ensured the stunt fails. And while the crash must be in the eye of the camera, the car or plane must miss the camera, if only by a hair's breadth. The camera outfits may cost £2,000 each, and it is not much good doing a stunt and smashing up valuable cameras as well."

In 1936 the squad is travelling the country, giving demonstrations of crazy driving and all manner of car stunting, driving through burning walls and sheets of glass, turning cars over at all speeds, each display ending with a full-speed crash and turnover.

Reg is also practising so that he can make an attempt in 1936 on the world's high altitude delayed parachute descent, which stands at 24,000 feet. He has achieved a drop of 16,800 feet but will try the 30,000 feet drop, which is rather more than five and a half miles. Last year when making a parachute descent at Brighton he fell into the sea and his water-logged parachute began to drag him under, and had not a life-saving expert been at hand the film industry would have lost the leader of the crash squad.

There is a definite price list for stunts, which naturally varies with conditions. Thus to crash an aeroplane into the sea demands a fee of £150; to change from plane to car or from car to plane, £75; an ordinary head-on crash in cars is £75, a head-on crash with one car overturned is £100, and with both cars overturned is £125. To crash an aeroplane into the tree tops is priced at £150, and a head-on collision between two planes in mid-air is worth £250. Most people would think that the crash squad value their lives very cheaply, for every crash involves a possibility of death.

A most excellent example of the work of Tom Purvis.

The whole thing is run on a business basis, the squad has offices in London, and owns four aeroplanes, eight high-powered motor cars, and twelve motorcycles, as well as two speed boats.

The films in which Reg and his squad can be seen to the best advantage are:-

Gaumont-British "Bulldog Jack", crash and turnover with car.

Gaumont-British "Forbidden Territory", lorry crash.

Radio picture " The Crouching Beast", doubling for Richard Bird in hectic and crazy driving, and acting as Fritz Kortner's chauffeur in crash and turnover.

"Air Trails", aeroplane crash and parachute descent.

A.T.P's "No Limit", crashes and daring high-speed motorcycling, including doubling for George Formby, who is himself a skilful motor-cyclist.

FROM A DRIVER'S VIEWPOINT – "THE OUTER CIRCUIT IS VALUABLE"
By C. T. Baker-Carr 1938

Brooklands Outer Circuit racing during the last two or three years has rather gone out of fashion. This is due to a variety of causes, the most obvious being the much greater publicity given to performances on the Donington, Crystal Palace and Brooklands road circuits.

It is fashionable for the non-competing fans of the sport to regard the Outer Circuit as a track of unnecessary width with no deviations, and where maximum speed is practically all that matters. At lap speed of about 110 miles per hour this is pretty true, but lapping at over 130 is a very different matter. The wide track immediately becomes a concrete road some 25 feet wide, and a very winding one at that. Banking does not

The French Societe Anonyme Theopile Schneider was formed in 1910 and embarked on an extensive competition campaign. The Company ceased manufacture in 1935.

straighten out the bend, but it does make it possible to get round so much quicker.

Supposing you are one of the back markers in a three-lap race, with a car which is handicapped to lap at over 130; to begin with, you can reckon that you have got to go absolutely flat-out the entire way to do any good at all.

Normally, for the first lap you are alone and can take your correct path, using as much of this comparatively narrow concrete road as you like. Then, suddenly, you find that you are catching one or two cars very quickly and they seem to be wandering about leaving you a doubtful gap to through. Simultaneously, you wonder how near you the scratch man has got. The cars just in front are travelling at 125, you at 135, and the man behind at 145.

What with a shower of concrete: your face, a mirror in which you can see nothing and no brakes, you have got your work cut out. Not so easy the first time out, nor the second for

the matter of that.

When lapping at 133 you get round in 75 seconds, which is a fairly short space of time for over 2½ miles. The only time during the lap you are able to pump up pressure, rest your arms; and check all the instrument readings is for about 25 seconds on the railway straight.

You go on to the Byfleet banking pretty low, where there is a nasty snake, and let the car wander up to its correct position at about the Hawker bridge. The Byfleet itself is fairly comfortable though rather hard work. You then pull the car down off the Byfleet early, get shot out of your seat and steer to within a couple of feet of the Vickers' sheds, hoping very much that a slower car just round the corner has not wandered over the black line leaving you no room.

Going on to the home banking, you have to persuade yourself to take higher than at first

The rarest mascot of them all? Reynard by Lalique c.1932.

you think is necessary, and then hold the car to its course as it tries to wander farther up. If you go on too low you find you shoot up immediately with most startling rapidity.

Having reached the members' bridge, you are beginning to accelerate again over the crest of the hill, and, as the curve of the banking here is not symmetrical, you have to cut the corner to bring the car square on to the big bump.

Inviolable Rule

Practically the only regulation on the Outer Circuit is that you shall keep to the left of your allotted line at the fork. This is a very strict rule, and it is religiously obeyed by even the most enthusiastic and excitable drivers. These particular people, however, seem to reckon that any other part of the circuit is free for all and their lack of imagination is astonishing.

However, it is all excellent experience for the driver, and that is where the outer circuit is so valuable. The newcomer to racing can make a very good beginning at the less important meetings organised by those very

nice people, the M.C.C. and J.C.C. When he is familiar with all the procedure which takes place during a race, he can then perform at a B.A.R.C. meeting in front of a large and critical audience, which is a little more nerve-racking.

The Main Essential

From then on, by steadily increasing his lap speeds, the driver can become perfectly familiar with conditions at high speed, which is the main essential to success. However much natural ability a man may have, until he is thoroughly at home at the speeds he has to use in a race, he is apt to be a danger to everyone.

Practice is of vital importance, but during a race the situation is incredibly different. This is particularly where the Outer Circuit makes it possible to gain the experience reasonably quickly and at relatively low cost. In short races on the road-circuits, unless you can afford an extremely expensive car, the usable maximum speeds are comparatively low.

The main difference between a fast road

circuit and the Brooklands Outer Circuit would seem to be primarily a lack of the use of brakes on the latter. It has become almost legendary that a car to be used on the Outer Circuit shall have its brakes made quite ineffective, but I can remember several occasions when they would have been very handy.

There has been a good deal of talk lately about the shortage of Outer Circuit cars. The Multi-Union proves that there is no such thing. Any road racing car which cannot lap the Outer Circuit at a speed in some relation to its maximum capabilities on the road is not the masterpiece of design most people imagine.

Treat the Outer Circuit as a very quick road circuit, put up some reasonable prize money, limit the engine size to about five litres, and there would be plenty of first-rate entries.

A short time ago there was a lot of correspondence in the motor papers as to who were our best drivers. Finally there was a ballot on the subject.

The correct order is impossible to sort out, but if anyone who was present at the B.A.R.C. Autumn Meeting ignores Chris Staniland, he must have been preoccupied in the bar. His win in the second race on the Outer Circuit was the finest bit of driving I have ever seen, bar none.

Successful Exponents

Almost immediately afterwards in the last race he gave a most magnificent display, leading a very select field on the Campbell Road Circuit until his brakes gave out. Staniland is an outstanding example of what can be got out of the Outer Circuit. For years he has lapped at 120 and 130, and now he gets a lightweight machine round at over 140. On the same car he won a road race in Ireland at no mean speed.

Drivers who have been successful on both the Outer Circuit and road circuits are Lord Howe, Charlie Dodson, Charles Martin, Freddie Dixon, Percy Maclure, and a great many others, not forgetting Tim Birkin.

It is all wrong that Outer Circuit racing and road racing should be regarded as entirely different forms of the sport. The finest drivers should be, equally good on both, as should be the best designed cars.

COUPE FLORIO BRESCIA 1907 — MINOïA sur ISOTTA-FRASCHINI

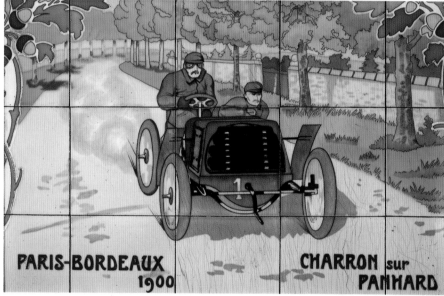

PARIS-BORDEAUX 1900 — CHARRON sur PANHARD

Plaster promotional figure of Monsieur Bibendum from America and dated 1910.

PARIS AMSTERDAM 1898 — CHARRON sur PANHARD

GRAND-PRIX Dieppe LAUTENSCHLAGER
de l'A·C·F· 1908 sur MERCÉDÈS

GRAND-PRIX Dieppe NAZZARO
de l'A·C·F· 1907 sur F·I·A·T·

The Michelin depot in South Kensington, London, the work of staff architect Francois Espinasse, complete with mechanically opening doors, mosaic flooring and the famous plaques depicting motor racing history was opened in 1910. This Art Nouveau building has now been restored and the racing panels live on, recalling motoring's Golden years.

COUPE GORDON-BENNETT THÉRY sur
1904 RICHARD-BRASIER

Gilardoni fils et Cᵉ
36 rue de Paradis-Paris

AFTERWORD

by Simon Khachadourian,
The Khachadourian Gallery, London.

Since the first spark fired the first automobile engine, artists, cartoonists, sculptors and designers have used the fine and decorative arts to celebrate, glorify, lampoon and promote the motor car. An appreciation of the motor car, and of motor racing, has been almost inseparable from an enthusiasm for automobile art, while the automotive and the advertising industries have come of age together, and have developed a mutual dependency.

My brother, Minas, inherited his enthusiasm for collecting from our father – a noted collector of manuscripts and paintings; in the case of Minas the passion manifested itself in the area of automobile art. At that time, there was little available in terms of reference material and no specialist auctions or galleries existed. As a result, considerable self-education was necessary, helped by contacts with like-minded enthusiasts. Nevertheless, my brother's collection grew steadily through the 1970s, leading to the opening of our first gallery, in London's Belgravia.

My own interest in the field was stimulated, inevitably, by the growing collection, and by the mid-70s my periodic forays into the market as an amateur dealer in automobile art were providing a welcome supplement to my income. By the early 80s, I had become a full-time dealer and collector; Minas and I combined our efforts, and expanded, in 1984, into the larger premises we now occupy in London's Pall Mall, near the Royal Automobile Club.

The Gallery has now established itself as the source for the much of the finest early and original material commercially available, and supplies a world-wide market. The visitor will find a wide range of automobile art, from original posters produced between 1890 and 1960 to automotive sculpture and trophies, oil paintings, prints and lithographs, as well as the Réné Lalique crystal car mascots of the 1920s and 1930s.

But our original enthusiasm as collectors continues undimmed, we still find it very satisfying to share our knowledge and expertise, both with established collectors and newcomers. Price, for example, is not necessarily an obstacle when it comes to starting a collection. One can still enter the market with a relatively small budget, although the dearest material, as in any field of collecting, will command substantial prices. This book illustrates material from all price levels, from inexpensive prints and lithographs to exceptional posters and sculptures, of which only a few examples are known to exist.

We are occasionally asked about the investment potential of automobile art. Generally, it is best to buy for appeal and interest rather than investment, though an investment potential certainly exists. As the market grows, the most desirable and rare material will become more scarce, and so more expensive.

One significant trend in recent years has been the interest shown by the automotive industries around in world in both sponsoring public museum collections of automobile art and developing corporate collections, and we have worked with several such groups. We anticipate further developments in this area, and believe that they can only serve to heighten public awareness and appreciation of automobile art in the long term.

As a Gallery, we also feel it important to create new material by commissioning talented contemporary artists to record the history of the motor car. We also give new life to existing material – to, for example, a limited edition of the famous ceramic tile panels that decorate Michelin House in London, arguably the most important examples of early automobile art. These historic scenes, some illustrated in this book, are now available to collectors both as ceramic panels and as art prints.

We have been delighted to provide the illustrations for MOTORING: THE GOLDEN YEARS. This fine book is a valuable addition to the literature and seems to us to be an ideal way of bringing the exciting world

REACHING FOR THE STARS

NANCY KERRIGAN
Olympic Figure Skater

Bob Italia

Published by Abdo & Daughters, 4940 Viking Drive, Suite 622, Edina, Minnesota 55435

Library bound edition distributed by Rockbottom Books, Pentagon Tower, P.O. Box 36036, Minneapolis, Minnesota 55435

Printed in the United States

Cover Photo credit: Bettmann
Interior Photo credits: Bettmann

Edited by Rosemary Wallner

Library of Congress Cataloging-in-Publication

Italia, Bob, 1955-
     Nancy, Kerrigan / Bob Italia : [edited by Rosemary Wallner].
        p. cm. --(Reaching for the Stars)
     ISBN 1-56239-339-1 (lib. bdg.)
     1. Kerrigan, Nancy, 1969-   --Juvenile Literature. 2. Women
skaters--United States--Biography--Juvenile Literature.
     [1. Kerrigan, Nancy, 1969-   2. Ice skaters. 3.Women--
Biography.] I. Wallner, Rosemary, 1964-   II. Title.
III. Series.
GV850.K38I83 1994
796.91 '2' 092--dc20   94-23382
     [B]   CIP
                                                          AC

TABLE OF CONTENTS

THE COMEBACK KID

As one of America's best figure skaters, Nancy Kerrigan was expected to challenge for gold medal honors at the upcoming Winter Games in Lillehammer, Norway. Though she finished with a silver medal, Kerrigan became famous the world over. But it wasn't because of her near-flawless performance in Lillehammer. Rather, her fame stemmed from one of the most bizarre events in Olympic history.

Fellow U.S. figure skater Tonya Harding was accused of plotting to injure Kerrigan before the Winter Games began. Kerrigan was assaulted, but rebounded in time to compete for a medal. She then went on to sign a lucrative contract with Disney that would secure her financially for the rest of her life.

Kerrigan wasn't the most talented figure skater ever. But in what became one of the greatest athletic comebacks ever, she persevered under incredible hardship and, through hard work and courage, nearly won the gold.

4

Figure skater Nancy Kerrigan won a silver medal at the 1994 Winter Olympics.

ALL IN THE FAMILY

A tight-knit family, the Kerrigans did everything together. They still live in the same two-story woodframe house where Nancy grew up. Kerrigan's grandparents, who live two doors away, often prepared Sunday breakfast for the extended family. And Kerrigan skated at the neighborhood rink, two blocks over, where her older brothers, Mark, 27, and Michael, 25, learned to play hockey.

Kerrigan first laced up at 6. She was a figure-skating star from the start, winning local, then regional championships. But the business of becoming a world-class skater was grueling—especially in her teens when Nancy had to get up at 4 A.M. to practice before going off to Stoneham High.

In 1970 Kerrigan's mother, Brenda, was at the wheel of her car when her vision suddenly went fuzzy. Afflicted with a rare virus, she gradually lost all sight in her left eye and most in her right. She is now legally blind.

Her children learned to adapt to her needs. They would leave notes for her in large block letters and pick up their rooms so

Brenda wouldn't trip over things left on the floor.

Household chores—shopping, cooking, laundry—were left to Nancy's father. It was he who drove her to beginner's classes at the local Stoneham rink in 1975.

When an instructor commented on Nancy's talent, the Kerrigans started her in private lessons they couldn't really afford. Dan worked extra jobs, took out loans and remortgaged the family home. Eventually the tab for Nancy's progress would soar to $50,000 a year. "Since Nancy started skating," says Dan, "the family hasn't been on a real vacation. We go to skating events."

Her parents' sacrifices, admitted Kerrigan, "made me feel guilty. I feel like everything they did was for me. It's scary when they are spending so much money and you don't know what you will get for it."

After graduating from Stoneham High in 1987, Nancy earned a two-year associate degree in business at nearby Emmanuel College. Under the tutelage of coach Evy Scotvold, she started entering—and medaling—in national competitions.

ALBERTVILLE

When she was 22, Nancy Kerrigan competed for an Olympic medal in Albertville, France. Together with Kristi Yamaguchi, 20, and Tonya Harding, 21, Kerrigan, who placed second at the nationals in Orlando, gave the U.S. its strongest women's team in years.

Kerrigan's mother, Brenda, was there at Albertville, but not in the stands. She was glued to a TV monitor. "I can't see someone's features unless I'm practically kissing them," said Brenda, who is blind in her left eye and has only marginal sight in her right. "I get right up close to the monitor, and I know if Nancy does a jump. But I don't know what kind of jump."

Whenever Kerrigan developed a new routine, she gave Brenda—and her dad, Daniel, 52—a preview in their Stoneham, Massachusetts, home. "I do it out on the floor in the living room," said Kerrigan, "with my arm movements, everything, so my mother can see it."

In 1991, the U.S. women's figure skating champions were (L to R) Tonya Harding, Kristi Yamaguchi and Nancy Kerrigan.

Kerrigan went on to win a bronze medal. Fame quickly followed her. Crowned by her hometown Boston Globe as "America's ice queen," Kerrigan was soon doing endorsements for Northwest Airlines, Reebok, Seiko and Campbell's soup. She was named one of PEOPLE'S 50 Most Beautiful People and made the cover of LIFE.

The problem was, her skating was falling apart.

"I just want to die," she said in Prague as she waited for her scores at the world championships. Her long program had been a disaster, dropping her to a fifth place finish. Her career in the post-Olympic season had gone, she said, "From poor to terrible to horrific."

Part of Nancy's problem, apparently, was that she simply couldn't stand prosperity. In the five years before the 1992 Olympics, she had always skated in the shadow of others—moving from 12th to second nationally.

But then she was expected to win. By June, her practice sessions with Scotvold had degenerated into protracted arguments. She objected to doing full run-throughs of her four-minute routine —not, she later realized, because she was lazy, but because she was frightened.

"I was really afraid to put my music on," she said. "If I wasn't perfect, I'd get at myself, put myself down." Things got so bad between skater and coach that Scotvold refused to instruct her for a month, turning her over to his wife, Mary.

Working with Boston sports psychologist Cindy Adams, Kerrigan said she dredged up a surprising insight: that she had always been motivated not by the possibility of success but by the fear of failure.

"It's kind of scary, giving everything you have," she recalled. "What if you're not as good as you think you are?"

Nancy Kerrigan practicing with her coach, Evy Scotveld.

In July, Kerrigan reapplied herself. She cut back on her personal appearances and trimmed down from 115 to 111 pounds. The new regimen paid off with a win in October, on the Olympic ice in Hamar, Norway, and at the AT&T Pro Am in Philadelphia. It was this new, improved Nancy Kerrigan whom she was eager to put on display at the nationals in Detroit.

THE ASSAULT

On January 6, 1994, while practicing for the national championships, Kerrigan was viciously attacked in Detroit's Cobo Arena by a club-wielding assailant who seemed to aim his blow deliberately at her knee.

A shaken Kerrigan watched from a skybox as longtime rival Tonya Harding finished first at the championships. She then returned to the sanctuary of her family home in Massachusetts to mend. An army of reporters camped outside her home, watching every move she made. The phone rang every three minutes. Kerrigan had nowhere to go. She was trapped, and bored with inactivity.

Down but undaunted, Kerrigan was eventually named to the 1994 U.S. Olympic team by the U.S. Figure Skating Association—displacing second-place finisher Michelle Kwan, 13, who graciously agreed with the decision.

Nancy Kerrigan became a product of the media. She couldn't go anywhere without a field of reporters following her every move.

THE PLOT UNFOLDS

Had it ended then, the incident might have been blamed on an unknown and deranged fan. But then an even darker scenario emerged. A minister in Portland, Oregon, reportedly told investigators that he had heard a tape in which three men were plotting to injure Kerrigan.

Who were these men? He said they were Tonya Harding's husband, Jeff Gillooly, her bodyguard, Shawn Eric Eckardt, and an unnamed hit man.

Harding herself was not implicated in the plot. Gillooly was quick to deny the charge. "I have more faith in my wife than to bump off the competition," said Gillooly.

Though no suspects had been charged by Wednesday evening, January 12, arrests were widely reported to be imminent. Stories circulated about an elaborate conspiracy hatched to knock Kerrigan out of the Olympic competition.

As it turned out, Kerrigan would find herself competing for the gold medal at the 1994 Winter Olympics in Lillehammer, Norway, on February 12. It was Tonya Harding whose career would forever be poisoned by the shocking attack in Cobo Arena.

PICKING UP THE PIECES

Meanwhile, Kerrigan tried to focus on the tasks at hand: rehabilitation and preparation. That meant getting rid of the fear that continued to stalk her.

"I was at a party Saturday night, and I was watching a little kid," Kerrigan said. "Suddenly I turned around, and there was someone standing with a bag of potato chips in their hand, which was close to my head when I turned. It scared me for a second—and I jumped."

When she returned to Stoneham, Kerrigan found a stack of mail on the hall table. Some of the envelopes were decorated with children's crayoned drawings.

Kerrigan read aloud from one of the letters: "We are so thankful you weren't harmed. We both know how difficult it can be to live in the public eye." It was signed by Nancy and Ronald Reagan.

That same afternoon, Kerrigan went to nearby Peabody, Massachusetts, to take a magnetic resonance imaging test to determine whether her knee had sustained serious damage. The test showed no hidden damage to the kneecap or muscles.

In a lengthy examination in his Salem, Massachusetts office later that day, Kerrigan's orthopedic surgeon, Dr. Bradley, pronounced the knee dramatically improved.

"Nancy has a 75-degree range of motion right now," said Bradley. "That is double the range she had at my last examination 24 hours ago."

But Kerrigan had to deal with psychological scars as well. She was ready for the challenge. "I've been a fighter all my life," she declared. "I think I'll be fine at Lillehammer, and I believe I will do great."

Nancy Kerrigan arrived in Lillehammer a week before everyone else so she could prepare. This photo shows her practicing at the Hamar arena.

For this, she had her parents to thank—particularly her mother. "I know my daughter," said Brenda. "I don't believe she needs any help to get over this. She's tough. She's strong. It's partly the way we brought her up. When she was a kid, there was a time when she had skates that were too small, and she would complain that her feet hurt. I used to say to her, 'Suffer in silence.' " And she did.

As details of the attack unfolded in the newspapers, Kerrigan read everything being written. When Kerrigan read about the bumblings of Stant, her assailant, she openly laughed. While stalking her, Stant had left his credit card in Phoenix, making it difficult for him to pay for anything like rooms, gas, and meals.

All this helped Kerrigan recover from the trauma of the assault. Believing that her attackers were idiots made them less terrifying.

The reporters outside her home were more frightening. So 13 days before the women's competition began, Kerrigan flew to Lillehammer, a good week earlier than most of her competitors would arrive.

But conditions at Lillehammer were almost as nightmarish as at home. Kerrigan's room in the Olympic Village in Hamar was tiny, almost cell-like. Her manager had forbidden her to go anywhere without a security guard. Kerrigan felt like a prisoner. In the Olympic Village cafeteria, Kerrigan was ogled by curious competitors. "Everyone would be looking at me like I was some sort of freak," Kerrigan said.

MORE BAD NEWS

When the news came on February 12 that the U.S. Olympic Committee, under the threat of a $25 million lawsuit, was dropping its disciplinary hearing and allowing Harding to compete in the Games, Kerrigan became livid. The FBI had been keeping the family informed of the criminal investigation. The Kerrigans had been led to believe that Harding might be arrested any day. Now Harding was going to be Kerrigan's teammate. Then the International Skating Union ruled that Harding and Kerrigan would have to practice together. All of Kerrigan's worst nightmares had come true.

U.S. figure skaters Nancy Kerrigan (R) and Tonya Harding pass by each other during a morning practice session at the Hamar Olympic arena.

By the time Harding arrived in Lillehammer on February 16, Kerrigan had gotten the anger out of her system. Kerrigan did not hug Harding when they finally met. But Kerrigan did say a few words to Harding before their first practice.

"Tough month for both of us, eh?" Kerrigan said.

"Yeah," Harding replied.

"Well," Kerrigan said, "I've got to get ready now."

Kerrigan was determined to prove she was just as tough as Harding. She could have easily moved out of her cubicle in the Olympic Village and stayed with her parents at a 19th-century manor. But Kerrigan didn't want it to look as if she were going out of her way to avoid contact with Harding.

Kerrigan did her best to enjoy the Olympics. She braved the crowds to take in two U.S. hockey games and to watch U.S. speedskaters Dan Jansen and Bonnie Blair each win gold medals. Kerrigan dined out every night with her manager.

On Wednesday, before she was to skate, Kerrigan finally inked her million-dollar deal with Disney, ensuring her economic future. As the competitors gathered in private to draw the starting order for the free skate, Harding startled Kerrigan by emerging from a group and hugging her quickly from the side. "Nancy looked stunned and anxious," said a witness.

Kerrigan was the 26th of 27 skaters to perform her short program. She felt a strange calm. It was different from anything else she had experienced.

"I felt a little too calm," she said. "I had to tell myself, 'All right, this is it. This is the Olympics.' "

Kerrigan did some sprints before lacing on her skates to get the adrenaline flowing. But when she took to the ice, her face still showed nothing but peace.

Oksana Baiul of Ukraine had been terrific. But Kerrigan bested her competition on this night. She skated a perfect technical program. Afterwards, with dozens of American flags waving, Kerrigan beamed proudly at center ice.

U.S. figure skater Nancy Kerrigan in action during her technical program, one of the events for women's Olympic figure skating.

The attack in Detroit had finally been pushed aside. One more night—the long program—and it would be all over.

On Friday night, Kerrigan gave the finest performance of her life. Though she doubled the opening triple flip, from that point on she was nearly flawless. It soon became evident to all that this was the best long program she ever skated. All that hard work paid off.

When the scores flashed on the board, revealing six 5.9s for artistic impression, it seemed certain that Kerrigan would win the gold medal. But Oksana Baiul of Ukraine snatched the gold medal away by the narrowest margin in Olympic history.

Baiul's balletic skate won five judges to Kerrigan's four. The German judge actually gave both competitors the same total score but awarded Baiul, the current world champion, the higher—and tie-breaking—artistic mark. China's Lu Chen won the bronze.

The stunning duel between the world's two premier female skaters was certainly a triumph for Kerrigan as well.

Medalists from the 1994 Winter Olympic women's free skate program (from left), Nancy Kerrigan (U.S.-Silver), Oksana Baiul (Ukraine-gold), and Lu Chin (China-bronze).

She performed with elegance, power and consistency—"a little bobble," she said, in her opening program, one simplified jump in her Friday-night free skate.

Kerrigan's silver medal capped perhaps the most dramatic comeback in sport's history. First she had to overcome the memory of a humiliating failure in the world championships in Prague. Then Kerrigan had to rebound from the vicious assault that knocked her out of the national championships.

There was some grumbling that Kerrigan's program—with its triple-jump combination—was more demanding, deserving higher technical marks at the very least. Kerrigan offered no complaint about the judging. "She'll have some initial disappointment," said her agent, Jerry Solomon, "and then be the happiest person alive. What she has accomplished in the last 60 days is remarkable."

"I was really proud of myself," said Kerrigan. "I thought I skated great."

Perhaps greatest of all, she left her nemesis, Tonya Harding, far behind.

Nancy Kerrigan appears to be flying through the air on her silver medal performance at the 1994 Winter Olympics.

Kerrigan exhibited beauty and grace both on and off the ice.

Harding, whose ex-husband had confessed to plotting the assault and had accused Harding of helping him, ceased to be counted among the world's elite skaters. She was never a factor in Norway.

OLYMPIC AFTERMATH

That Kerrigan didn't strike gold would soon be forgotten by adoring American audiences—the ladies' competition played to more than 100 million TV viewers—who would see Nancy on a succession of major ad campaigns and entertainment projects.

Meanwhile, Tonya Harding pleaded guilty March 16, 1994, in Portland, Oregon, to a conspiracy charge stemming from the January 6 assault on Kerrigan. Harding's plea came as part of an agreement with prosecutors.

As part of an agreement, Jeff Gillooly, in February, had pleaded guilty to racketeering in connection with organizing the attack. Gillooly awaited sentencing on that count. Three other men were indicted in the attack March 21.

Harding pleaded guilty to a charge of hindering the investigation of the attack stemming from her initial failure to tell authorities what she knew about the incident. In entering her plea, she admitted to conspiring with Gillooly and her former bodyguard, Shawn E. Eckardt, to cover up the plot. However, Harding continued to deny foreknowledge of the plan.

Under the terms of her plea agreement, she received three years' probation and was fined $100,000, but was guaranteed no prison time. The skater agreed to establish a $50,000 fund for Special Olympics in Oregon and to re-emburse the county prosecutor's office $10,000 in legal costs. Harding also agreed to undergo a psychiatric evaluation and to perform 500 hours of community service.

As part of the agreement, Harding was to resign from the U.S. Figure Skating Association, thereby ending her amateur skating career. She was to also withdraw from competing on the U.S. team in world championships in Chiba, Japan, which began March 20. (Harding was replaced by alternate Nicole Bobek.)

A grand jury in Portland, March 21, indicted three men who had confessed to their involvement in the attack on Kerrigan. The grand jury also accused Harding of involvement in the plot. However, Harding could not be indicted due to her earlier plea agreement.

The three indicted suspects were Eckardt, who had admitted to planning the assault, Shane M. Stant, who acknowledged executing the assault, and Derrick B. Smith, who confessed to being the getaway-car driver.

All three men pleaded not guilty to charges of racketeering, conspiracy to commit assault, second-degree assault and unlawfully obtaining communications. The last charge stemmed from a tape-recorded meeting.

Eckardt was indicted on additional charges of conspiracy to hinder prosecution and hindering prosecution. Smith was also charged with conspiracy to hinder prosecution.

According to the indictment, the conspirators had defrauded the USFSA, using funds the association had earmarked for training costs in order to hire Stant and Smith to carry out the assault.

A SPECIAL PERSON

Twenty-four hours after she had won her silver medal, the Kerrigan's waited to board a plane bound for home. Brenda was still disappointed with the outcome. But she looked upon it in a new and a more favorable light.

"It's not right, what the judges did, but they did us a favor," she said. "The silver medal will give Nancy back her normal life quicker. They did us a favor. Nancy, you know, never liked being special."

Considering that she engineered one of the greatest comebacks in professional sports, "special" is the best word to describe Nancy Kerrigan.

Nancy Kerrigan, Olympic figure skating star.